Just Swimming Around

(Pages 5 and 6)
Directions for two players:

1. Cut off the answer key below and put it aside.
2. Choose a different-colored pencil than your partner.
3. Use a pencil and a paper clip to spin the spinner on your other page. Read the question in the section where the spinner stops.
4. Point to an adjective on the gameboard that answers the question. Have your partner check your answer with the key. If your answer is correct, color that fish on the gameboard. If the answer is incorrect or there are no uncolored fish left that answer the question, your turn is over.
5. The player with more colored fish when all the fish are colored wins.

Answer Key for "Just Swimming Around"

Which One(s)	What Kind	How Many
that	round	few
these	blue	many
this	colorful	one
those	fragile	six
	orange	some
	shallow	thousand
	tiny	
	vibrant	
	warm	

Just Swimming Around

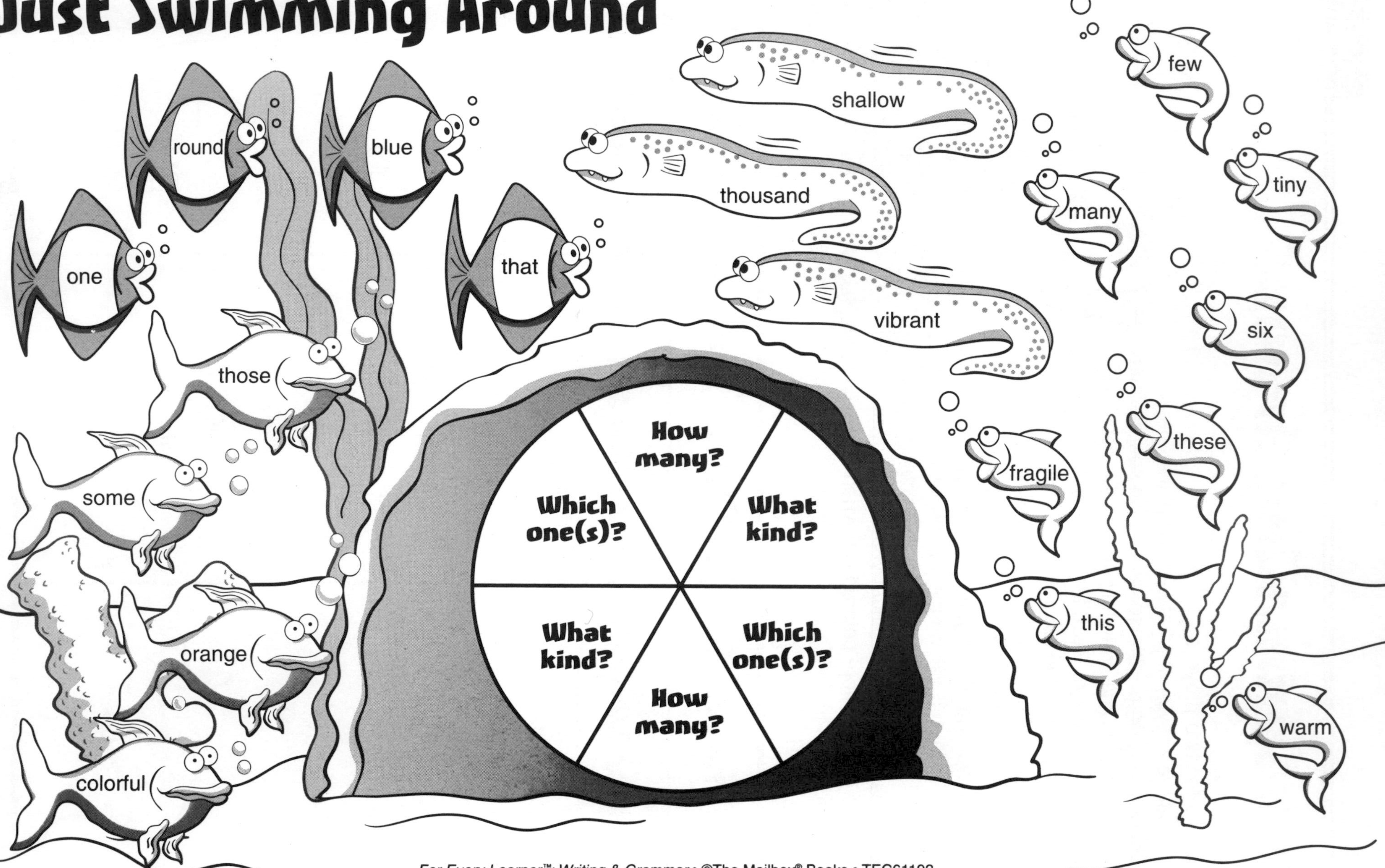

one
round
blue
that
those
some
orange
colorful
shallow
thousand
vibrant
few
tiny
many
six
these
fragile
this
warm

How many?
What kind?
Which one(s)?
How many?
What kind?
Which one(s)?

Note to the teacher: Use with "Just Swimming Around" on page 5.

We Want to Vote!

Circle the adjective or adjectives in each sentence.
In the table below, make a tally mark for each type of adjective you find.
If the total matches the number of the amendment that granted women the right to vote, you found them all!

1. Women in the 1800s had few rights compared to men.
2. When any woman got married, the husband would then own all property she had.
3. Most colleges would not admit any females.
4. Women could not vote in local, state, or national elections.
5. Some women thought they could do nothing to change this way of thinking.
6. Then several women arranged a special meeting in New York to discuss the unfair matter.
7. Starting with that meeting, popular support for giving women equal rights began to build.
8. In 1920, the 19th amendment was added to the Constitution of the United States.
9. This amendment gave women the important right to vote.

Which One(s)	What Kind	How Many

Total number of adjectives: ______

An Eye for Adjectives

1. Cut apart the cards below.
2. Glue the four heading cards to another sheet of paper as shown.
3. Glue the word cards under the corresponding headings.
4. On a sheet of notebook paper, write a sentence that includes at least one word from each section. Repeat until you have written as many sentences as you can.

What Kind		Which One(s)	
How Many		Not an Adjective	
crunchy	miniature	green	those
cheerfully	these	three	some
hungrily	steep	this	several
two	noisy	anxiously	three-sided
friendly	brisk	50	amazing
that	France	nine	America

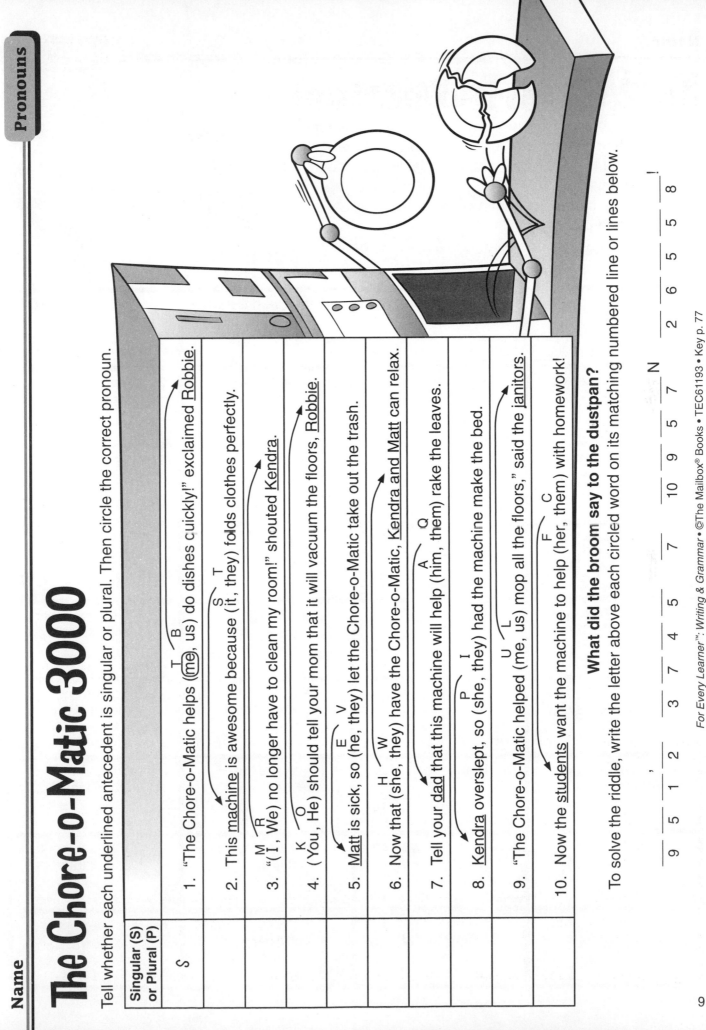

Name

The Chore-o-Matic 3000

Tell whether each underlined antecedent is singular or plural. Then circle the correct pronoun.

Singular (S) or Plural (P)	
S	1. "The Chore-o-Matic helps (T me, B us) do dishes cuickly!" exclaimed <u>Robbie</u>.
	2. This <u>machine</u> is awesome because (S it, T they) folds clothes perfectly.
	3. "(M I, R We) no longer have to clean my room!" shouted <u>Kendra</u>.
	4. (K You, O He) should tell your mom that it will vacuum the floors, <u>Robbie</u>.
	5. <u>Matt</u> is sick, so (E he, V they) let the Chore-o-Matic take out the trash.
	6. Now that (H she, W they) have the Chore-o-Matic, <u>Kendra and Matt</u> can relax.
	7. Tell your <u>dad</u> that this machine will help (A him, Q them) rake the leaves.
	8. <u>Kendra</u> overslept, so (P she, I they) had the machine make the bed.
	9. "The Chore-o-Matic helped (U me, L us) mop all the floors," said the <u>janitors</u>.
	10. Now the <u>students</u> want the machine to help (F her, C them) with homework!

What did the broom say to the dustpan?

To solve the riddle, write the letter above each circled word on its matching numbered line or lines below.

__ __ __'__   __ __ __ __   __   __ __ __ __N   __ __ __ __ __!
9 5 1 2   3 7 4 5   7   10 9 5 7   2 6 5 5 8

Name

The World Traveler

1. Cut out the cards. Then group the cards by number.
2. In each group of cards, form a complete sentence by matching the two cards whose underlined pronoun and antecedent agree.
3. Place the card pairs in numerical order to reveal a riddle and its answer.
4. Glue the card pairs, in order, to a sheet of paper.

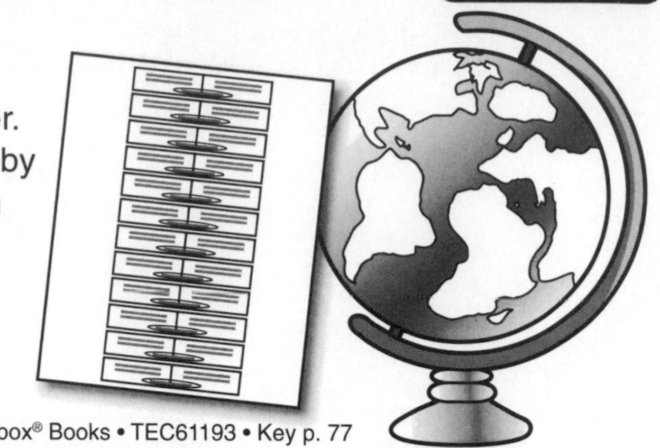

1. The basketball bounces, (WH)	10. replied the players. (NER?)	5. me guard the other team's star player." (LD)	12. "You are the best!" (STA)
3. so the coach relies on him. (UND)	6. and shout about it. (UT)	7. so she tells the others what to do. (AYS)	2. hard, and we support them. (VELS)
4. She is the team's (T)	7. so he tells the others what to do. (IR)	6. and shout about them. (E)	12. "We are the best!" (GLI)
8. "She hopes we do well (O)	2. The players on the team practice (TRA)	7. Britney is the head cheerleader, (ST)	10. "I am the one who should be nervous," (OW)
3. Roger is the star of the team, (ARO)	4. biggest fan. (HE)	11. Robert and the other players worked (A POST)	5. I guard the other team's star player." (RY)
6. The cheerleaders bring team spirit (B)	1. and the players dribble them. (ERE)	9. "You have nothing to worry about, (ON)	9. "She has nothing to worry about, (H)
11. hard, and they won. (AGE)	5. Robert said, "Help (WOR)	4. They are the team's (S)	2. hard, and we support him. (CK)
9. Britney," said Robert. (E)	11. hard, and we won. (ER)	1. and the players dribble it. (AT)	12. the crowd shouted to the team. (MP)
10. "We are the ones who should be nervous," (COR)	8. during the game today," said Britney. (N)	3. so the coach relies on her. (MA)	8. "I hope we do well (I)

Just Jousting

(Pages 11 and 12)

1. Write your name on the blank card below. Then cut out the cards.
2. Use a pencil and a paper clip to spin the spinner on your other page.
3. Use the pronoun you land on and an antecedent card to write a sentence in the space provided. Draw an arrow from the pronoun to its antecedent. Repeat until you have completed six sentences.
4. Answer the question to explain your thinking.

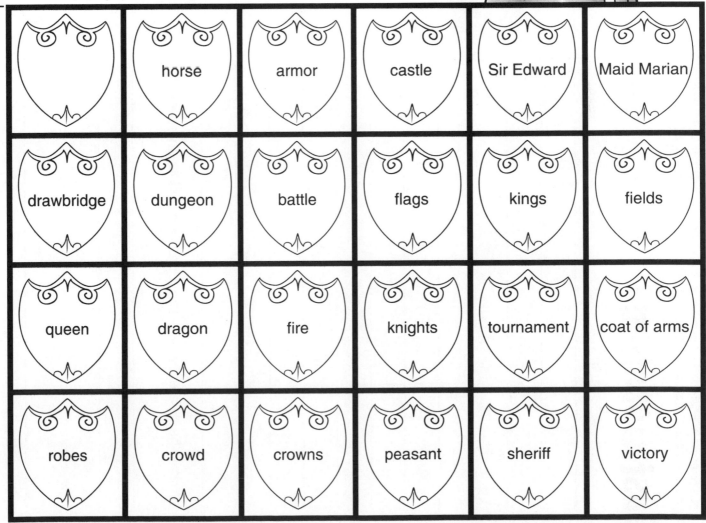

	horse	armor	castle	Sir Edward	Maid Marian
drawbridge	dungeon	battle	flags	kings	fields
queen	dragon	fire	knights	tournament	coat of arms
robes	crowd	crowns	peasant	sheriff	victory

Just Jousting

1. ______________________________

2. ______________________________

3. ______________________________

4. ______________________________

5. ______________________________

6. ______________________________

them I you we us he she it me they him her

7. What is the difference between a pronoun and its antecedent?

____

Note to the teacher: Use with "Just Jousting" on page 11.

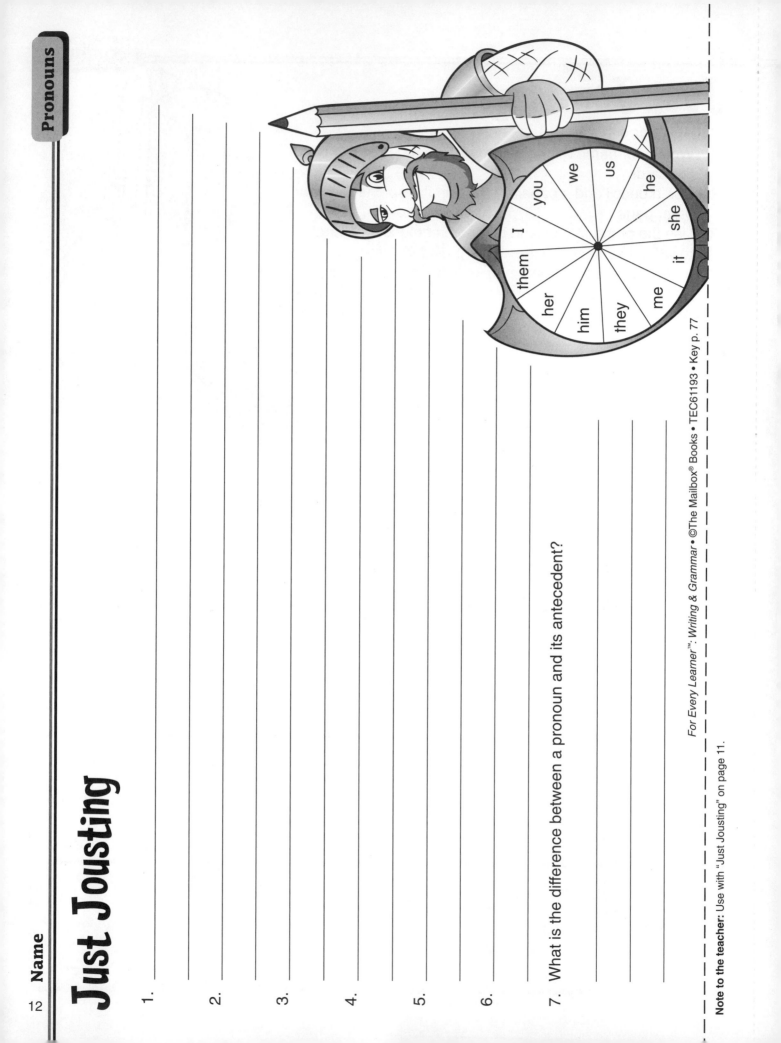

X Marks the Spot

1. Cut out the cards below.
2. Sort the cards by correct and incorrect sentences.
3. Fix each incorrect sentence.
4. Arrange the incorrect cards to reveal a treasure map. Glue the map to another sheet of paper.

For Every Learner™: Writing & Grammar • ©The Mailbox® Books • TEC61193 • Key p. 77

Argh! Find our treasure, and become rich!	 The kids find an old mysterious message in a bottle.	We are packing shirts, shorts, and sandals for our trip.
Follow, Hunt, The ship leaves on Saturday July 4 for Cancun Mexico.	Anne finds a map that is titled *Follow Hunt, and Find.*	 Anne, Bart, and Jack then find a glowing golden treasure!
Bart, the youngest of the three does not understand.	Jack however reaches land first.	**and Find** Anne Bart and Jack are getting bored on the ship.
First, swim to the island to find your next clue.	Anne take your brothers on an adventure.	The kids find a raft jump in the water, and swim.

Comma Drama

(Pages 14 and 15)

1. Cut out the cards below.
2. Read each sentence on your other page.
3. Tape a card showing a smiling face on each correct sentence.
4. Tape the top of the appropriate rule card on each incorrect sentence. Then lift the rule card and correct the sentence using the rule. Some cards will not be used.
5. Once all sentences have been covered, check to see that you have four matching cards in a row.

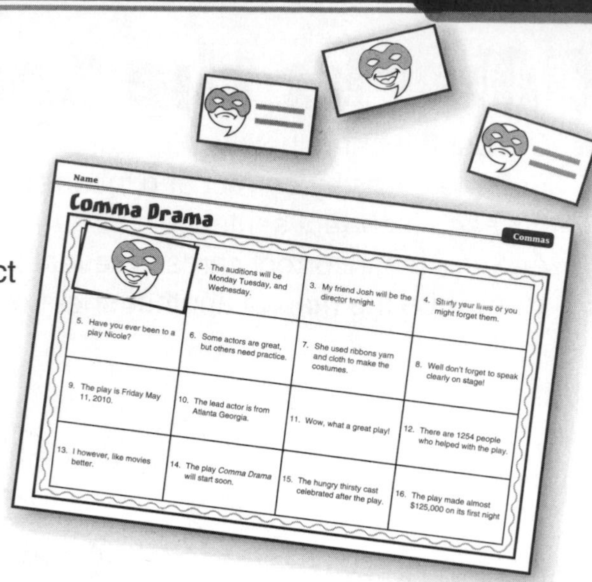

For Every Learner™: Writing & Grammar • ©The Mailbox® Books • TEC61193 • Key p. 77

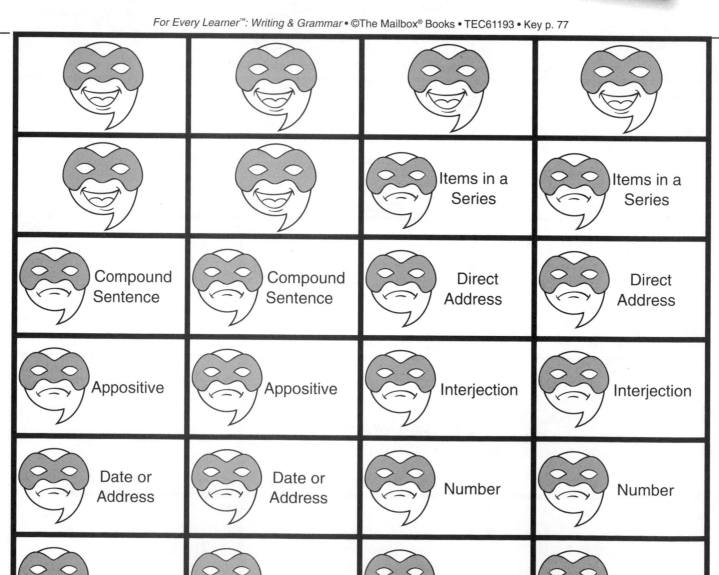

		Items in a Series	Items in a Series
Compound Sentence	Compound Sentence	Direct Address	Direct Address
Appositive	Appositive	Interjection	Interjection
Date or Address	Date or Address	Number	Number
Interruption	Interruption	Adjectives	Adjectives

Name

Comma Drama

1. Kyle, will you be acting in the play?	2. The auditions will be Monday Tuesday, and Wednesday.	3. My best friend Josh will be the director tonight.	4. Study your lines or you might forget them.
5. Have you ever been to a play Nicole?	6. Some actors are great, but others need practice.	7. She used ribbons yarn and cloth to make the costumes.	8. Well don't forget to speak clearly on stage!
9. The play is Friday May 11, 2010.	10. The lead actor is from Atlanta Georgia.	11. Wow, what a great play!	12. There are 1254 people who helped with the play.
13. I however, like movies better.	14. The first play *Comma Drama* will start soon.	15. The hungry thirsty cast celebrated after the play.	16. The play made almost $125,000 on its first night.

Note to the teacher: Use with "Comma Drama" on page 14.

Close-Up!

Write a sentence in each set of boxes. Write only one word in each box, and pay attention to the placement of the commas.

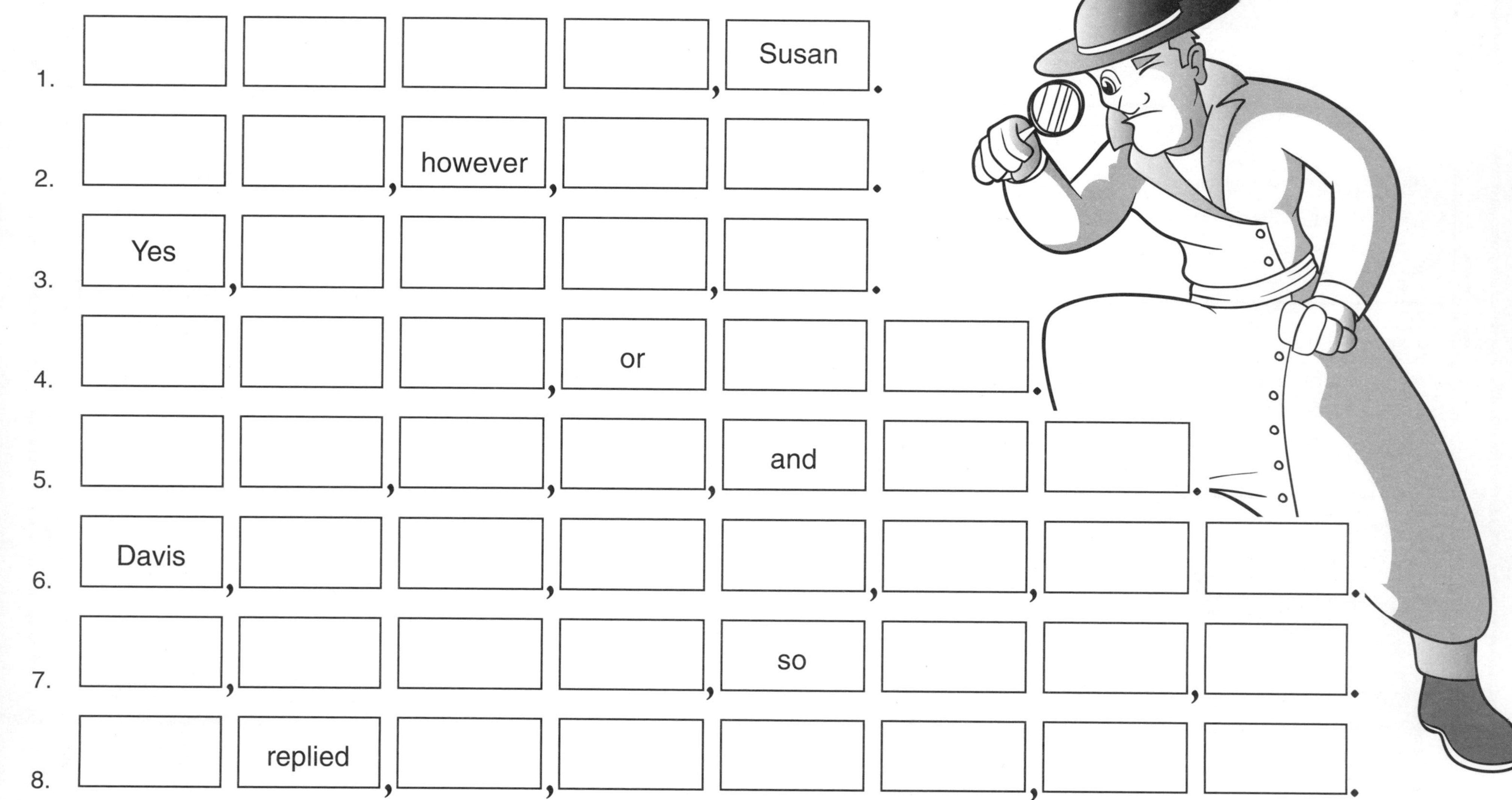

1. ☐ ☐ ☐ ☐, Susan.
2. ☐ ☐, however, ☐ ☐.
3. Yes, ☐ ☐ ☐, ☐.
4. ☐ ☐ ☐, or ☐ ☐.
5. ☐ ☐, ☐, ☐, and ☐ ☐.
6. Davis, ☐ ☐, ☐ ☐, ☐, ☐ ☐.
7. ☐, ☐ ☐ ☐, so ☐ ☐, ☐.
8. ☐ replied, ☐, ☐ ☐ ☐, ☐ ☐.

Name

Tickle Your Funny Bone!

1. Add quotation marks around each speaker's words on the strips below.
2. Cut apart the strips.
3. Sort them to form eight different jokes.
4. Glue each set of strips to another sheet of paper.

Do you want a horn on your saddle? asked the rancher.	So I can finish before my pen runs out of ink, replied the student.
What do you get when you cross a pig with a frog? asked the nature guide.	An accountant, answered Larry.
If two rights don't make a wrong, asked Wilbur, what do two rights make?	I wish you wouldn't ask me, replied the waiter. I don't know one bug from another.
Why are you writing so fast? asked the teacher.	A 'ham-phibian,' answered a young boy.
A customer asked, What is this insect in my soup?	No. There doesn't seem to be much traffic out here, replied the cowboy.
How are spiders like tops? asked a child.	Because, answered her mom, they sell what they knead.
What kind of ant is good at adding numbers? asked Barry.	They are always spinning! exclaimed the child's big brother.
Sheila asked, Why are bakers silly?	An airplane! exclaimed Orville.

Who's Who?

(Pages 18 and 19)

1. Look at the name bank. Write each name on its matching card below.
2. Add quotation marks where they are needed.
3. Cut apart the cards.
4. Glue each card in its matching box on your other page.

Name Bank

Walt Disney	Thomas Edison	Benjamin Franklin	Patrick Henry
Michael Jordan	Martin Luther King Jr.	Babe Ruth	Charles Schulz

Every strike brings me closer to the next home run, reported ______________________.

Never leave that till tomorrow which you can do today, advised ______________________.

I've missed more than 9,000 shots in my career. I've lost almost 300 games. Twenty-six times, I've been trusted to take the game-winning shot and missed. I've failed over and over and over again in my life. And that is why I succeed, said ______________________.

I have not failed. I've just found 10,000 ways that won't work, explained ______________________.

All our dreams can come true, if we have the courage to pursue them, stated ______________________.

I have a dream that my four little children will one day live in a nation where they will not be judged by the color of their skin, but by the content of their character, said ______________________.

If you're going to draw a comic strip every day, commented ______________________, you're going to have to draw on every experience in your life.

I know not what course others make take, exclaimed ______________________, but as for me: give me liberty, or give me death.

Name

Who's Who?

Note to the teacher: Use with "Who's Who?" on page 18.

Name

Let's Talk!

These students are on the phone talking about their school project. Use the thoughts below to write what they are saying to each other.

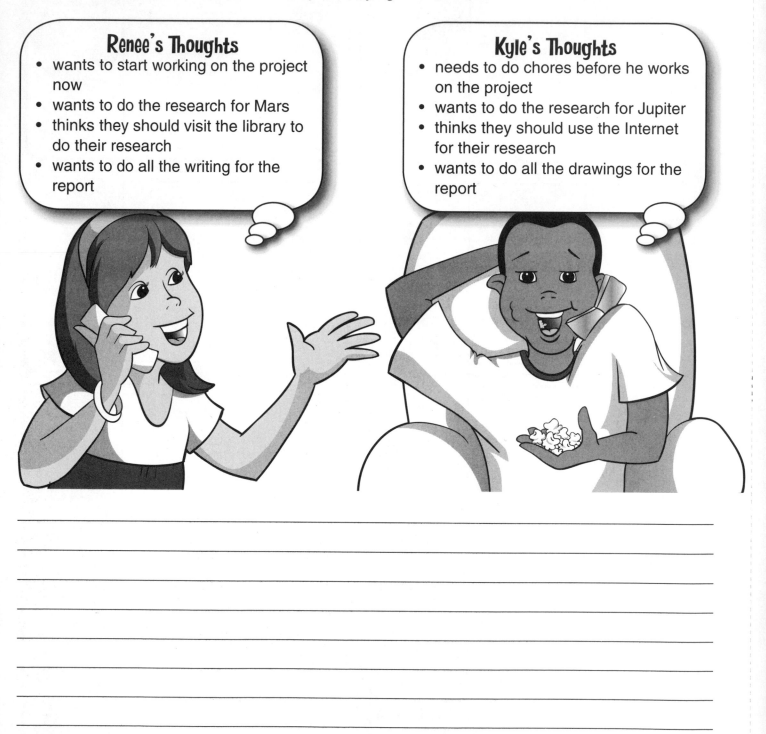

Renee's Thoughts

- wants to start working on the project now
- wants to do the research for Mars
- thinks they should visit the library to do their research
- wants to do all the writing for the report

Kyle's Thoughts

- needs to do chores before he works on the project
- wants to do the research for Jupiter
- thinks they should use the Internet for their research
- wants to do all the drawings for the report

Use the back if you need more space.

Don't Miss the Bus!

(Pages 21 and 22)

1. Cut out the sentence cards below.
2. Add the missing punctuation to each card.
3. Sort and glue the cards on your other page.

For Every Learner™: Writing & Grammar • ©The Mailbox® Books • TEC61193 • Key p. 78

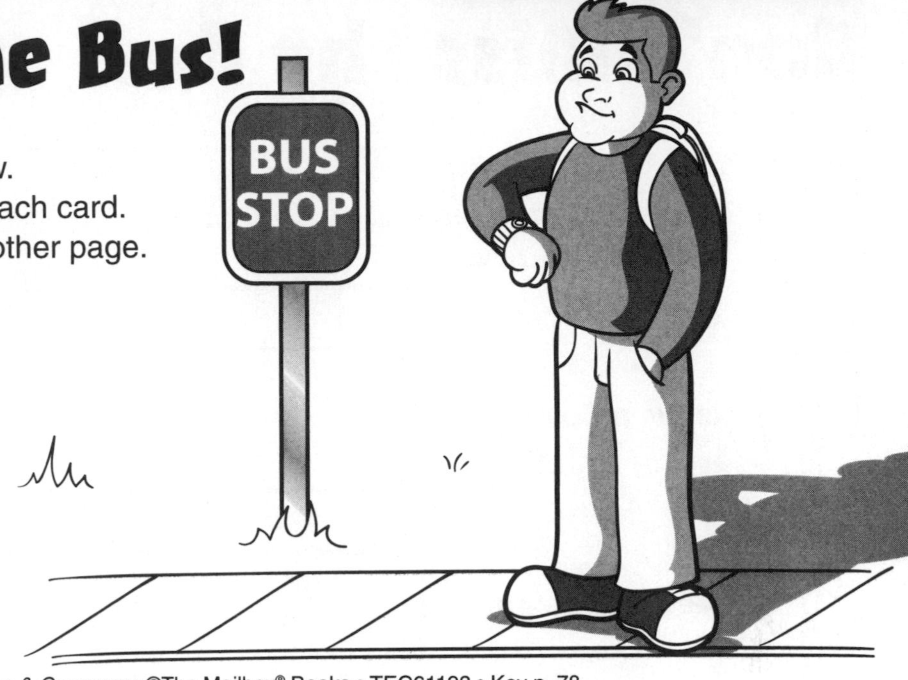

"If you dont wake up, youre going to miss the bus!" Mom shouted.

I hope the school bus is running late today; otherwise, I might miss it, Wally stated.

Every morning I grab my backpack, which holds my homework; grab my lunch and run to the bus.

At the bus stop many kids talk and tell jokes.

On average, how many students ride the school bus every day

"My favorite T shirt is school bus yellow," Wally said.

My school bus can be described as the following loud, fun, smelly, crowded, and stuffy.

Have you ever read the book 101 Ways to Pass the Time on a School Bus?

Name

Don't Miss the Bus!

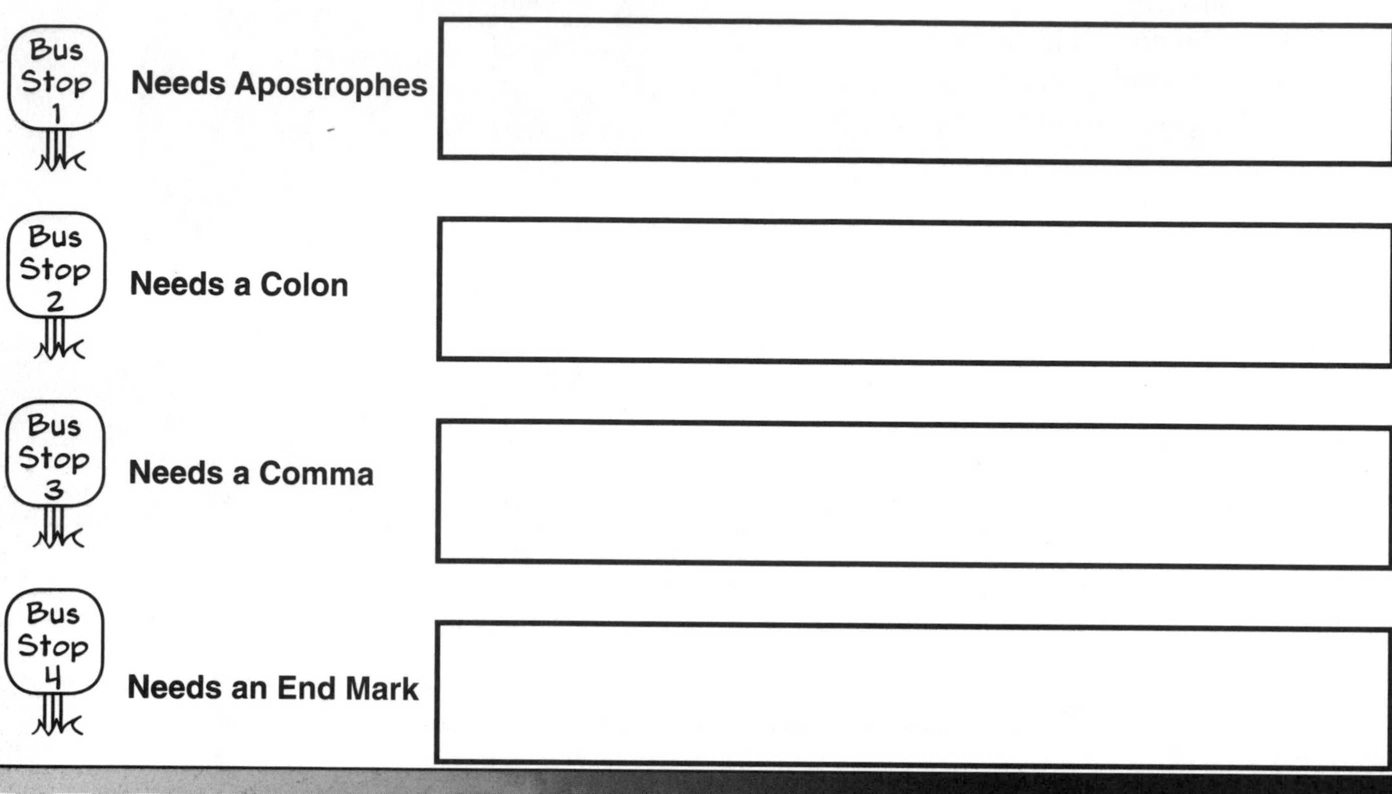

Needs a Hyphen — Bus Stop 5

Needs Quotation Marks — Bus Stop 6

Needs a Semicolon — Bus Stop 7

Needs Underlining or Italics — Bus Stop 8

Note to the teacher: Use with "Don't Miss the Bus!" on page 21.

Name

Sweet Sentences

1. Cut out the sentence box and each punctuation mark below.
2. Read each sentence in the box.
3. Rewrite each sentence on a large sheet of construction paper, gluing the correct punctuation where needed.

Sentences

1. Marias favorite candy includes the following bubble gum jawbreakers and licorice Abby explained
2. To get to the candy store make a U turn at the end of Poplar Grove Road
3. Candy A Sweet Guide is my favorite book Maria exclaimed
4. Abby replied I like candy I however like fruits and vegetables better
5. What How can you not like candy more than anything else
6. When you eat candy you also must brush your teeth frequently
7. Ive been eating candy since I can remember and I dont plan to stop anytime soon
8. How many cavities do you have Abby asked

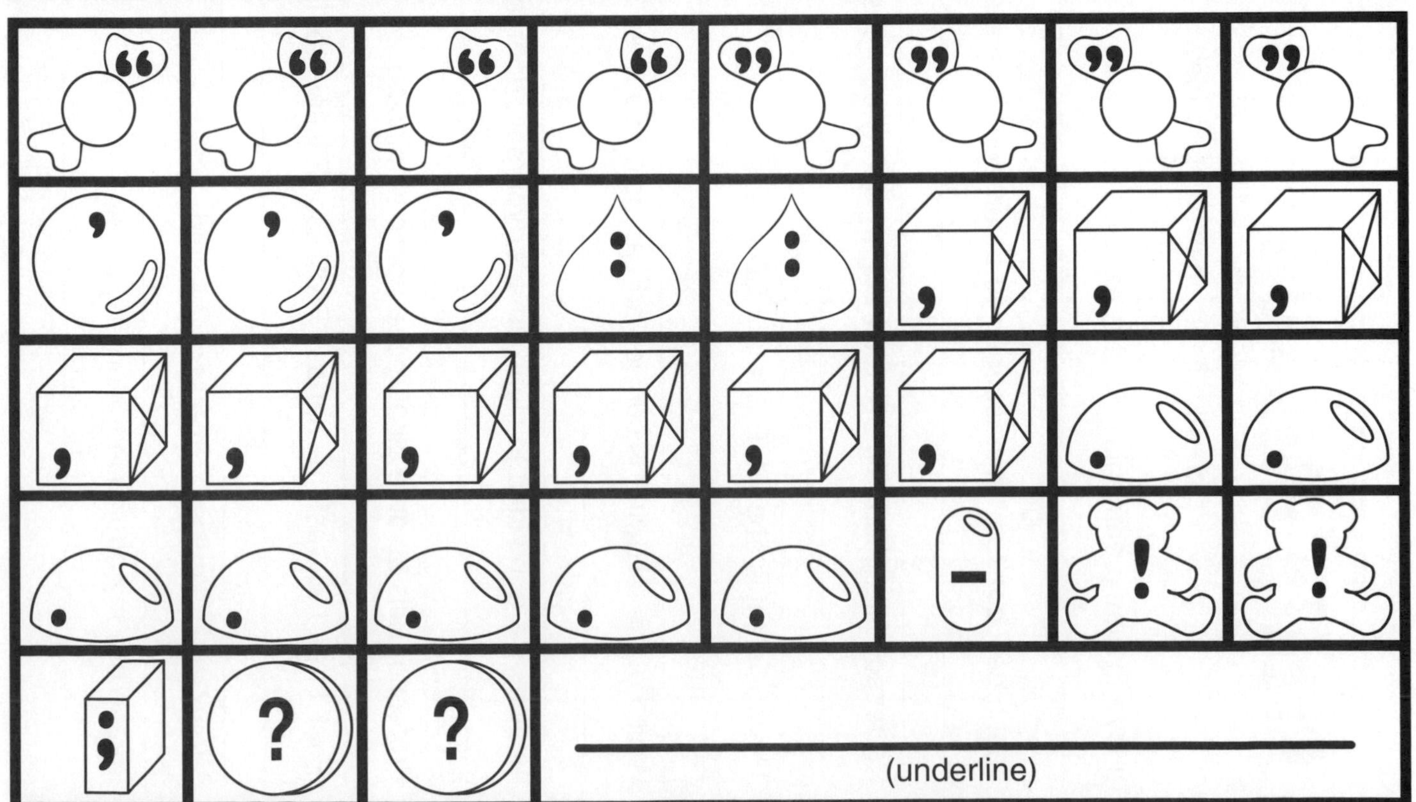

A Little Mix-Up

Rewrite each sentence correctly. Then answer the question.

1. :I love to do experiments?: Professor Bill exclaimed”
2. Test tubes’ beakers’ microscopes’ and compounds are all over his messy lab.
3. Professor Bill asked’ :Where did I put my safety goggles!:
4. The assistant is absent, Professor Bill needs help”
5. Which of the following is correct; add an acid to a base or add a base to an acid!
6. Its always a good idea to clean up after yourself, dont leave a mess.
7. Professor Bills favorite all:purpose apron is missing.
8. :First’ I need to wash my hands’: Professor Bill said :before I start the experiment.:
9. :Wow? what a mess?: Professor Bill said!
10. Please buy my book titled “Running a Lab Smoothly.”

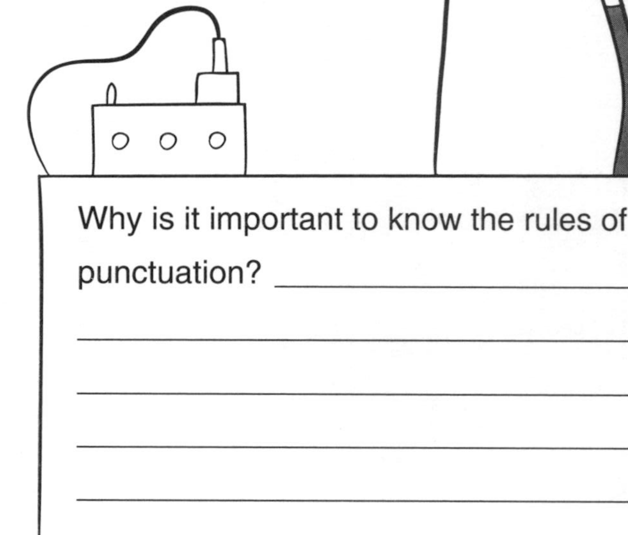

Why is it important to know the rules of punctuation?

Name

Ride of Your Life

1. Cut apart the cards below and place them facedown in rows.
2. Turn over two cards. If they agree and make sense together, write a sentence on a sheet of paper using the pair. Then set the cards aside. If they do not agree or make sense, turn the cards facedown.
3. Continue in this way until all cards have been used in a sentence.

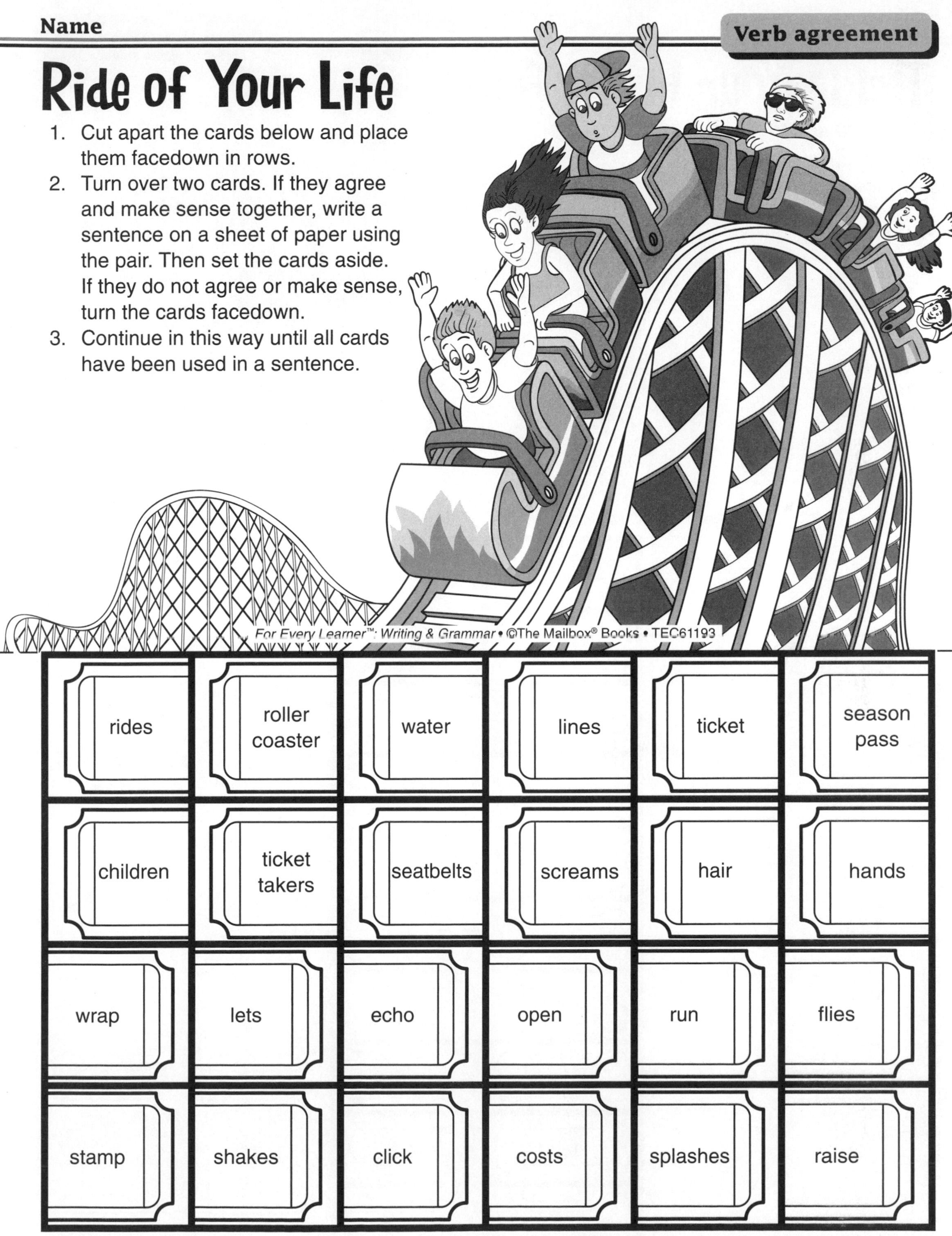

rides	roller coaster	water	lines	ticket	season pass
children	ticket takers	seatbelts	screams	hair	hands
wrap	lets	echo	open	run	flies
stamp	shakes	click	costs	splashes	raise

Tickle Your Funny Bone

(Pages 26 and 27)

1. Cut out the cards below.
2. Use the cards to complete each joke on your other page. Not all cards will be used.
3. Glue each card in place.

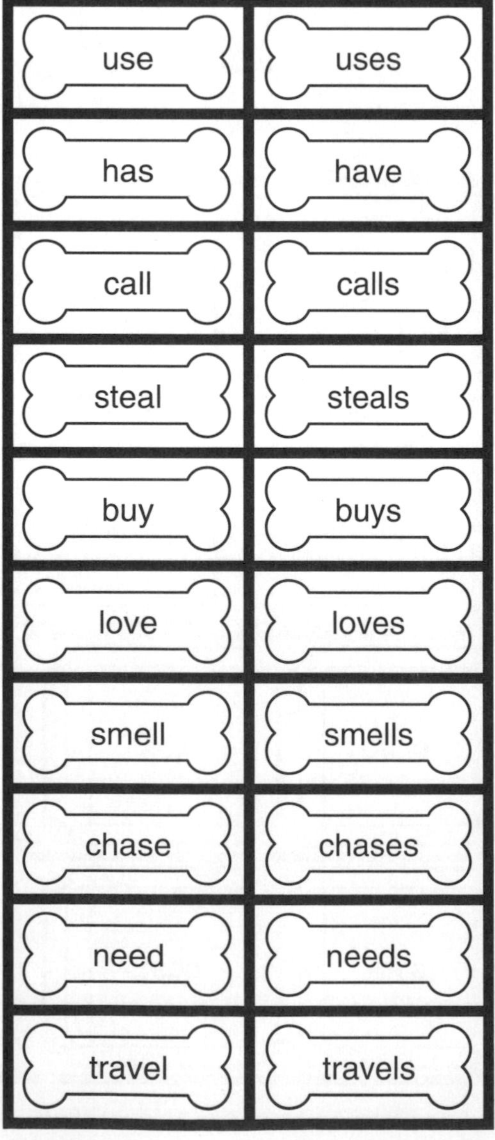

use
uses
has
have
call
calls
steal
steals
buy
buys
love
loves
smell
smells
chase
chases
need
needs
travel
travels

Name

Tickle Your Funny Bone

1. What kind of dog [ ] like onions? A hot dog

2. What do people do when a dog gets sick? They [ ] a "dog-tor."

3. Where do dogs buy their clothes? Dogs [ ] them at K-9 Mart.

4. How does the magician make a puppy disappear? He [ ] Spot remover.

5. Why is the dog sent out of the flea circus? Because he [ ] the show

6. Why is the dog jealous of the tree? Because the tree [ ] better bark

7. What dogs [ ] to take baths? "Shampoo-dles"

8. On what kind of bus do fleas [ ] ? A Greyhound bus

9. What does a lazy dog do? It [ ] parked cars.

10. A dog [ ] hair. Why? So that it's not a little bear

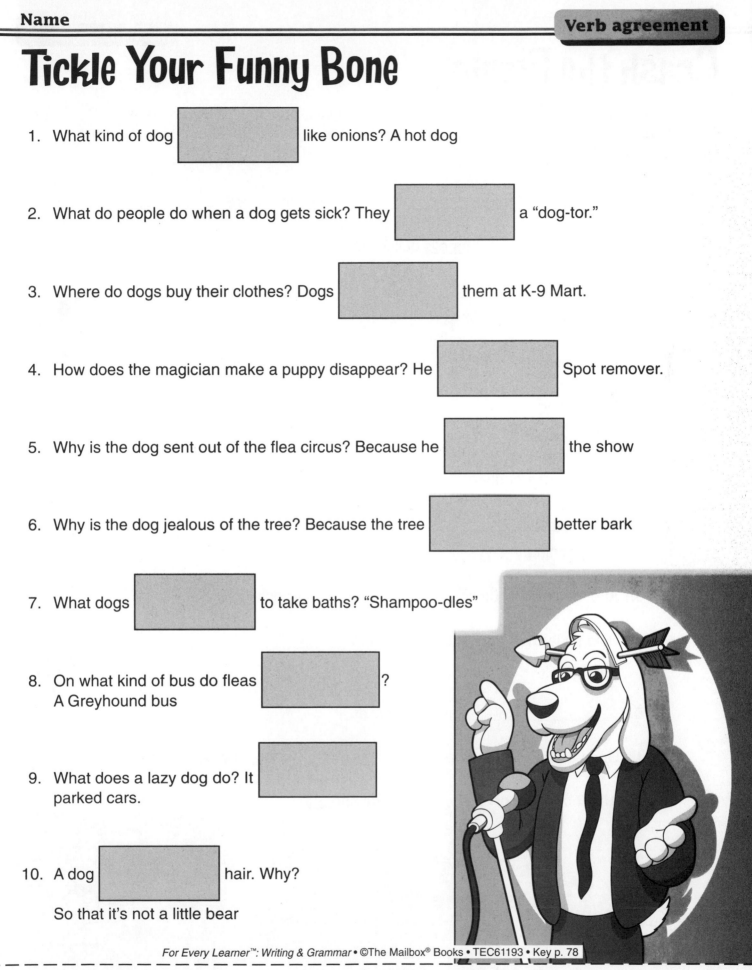

Note to the teacher: Use with "Tickle Your Funny Bone" on page 26.

Name

Crash the Picnic

Decide whether each underlined subject or verb is singular or plural. Above each, write *S* if it is singular or *P* if it is plural. Then complete each sentence using either a subject or a verb that agrees.

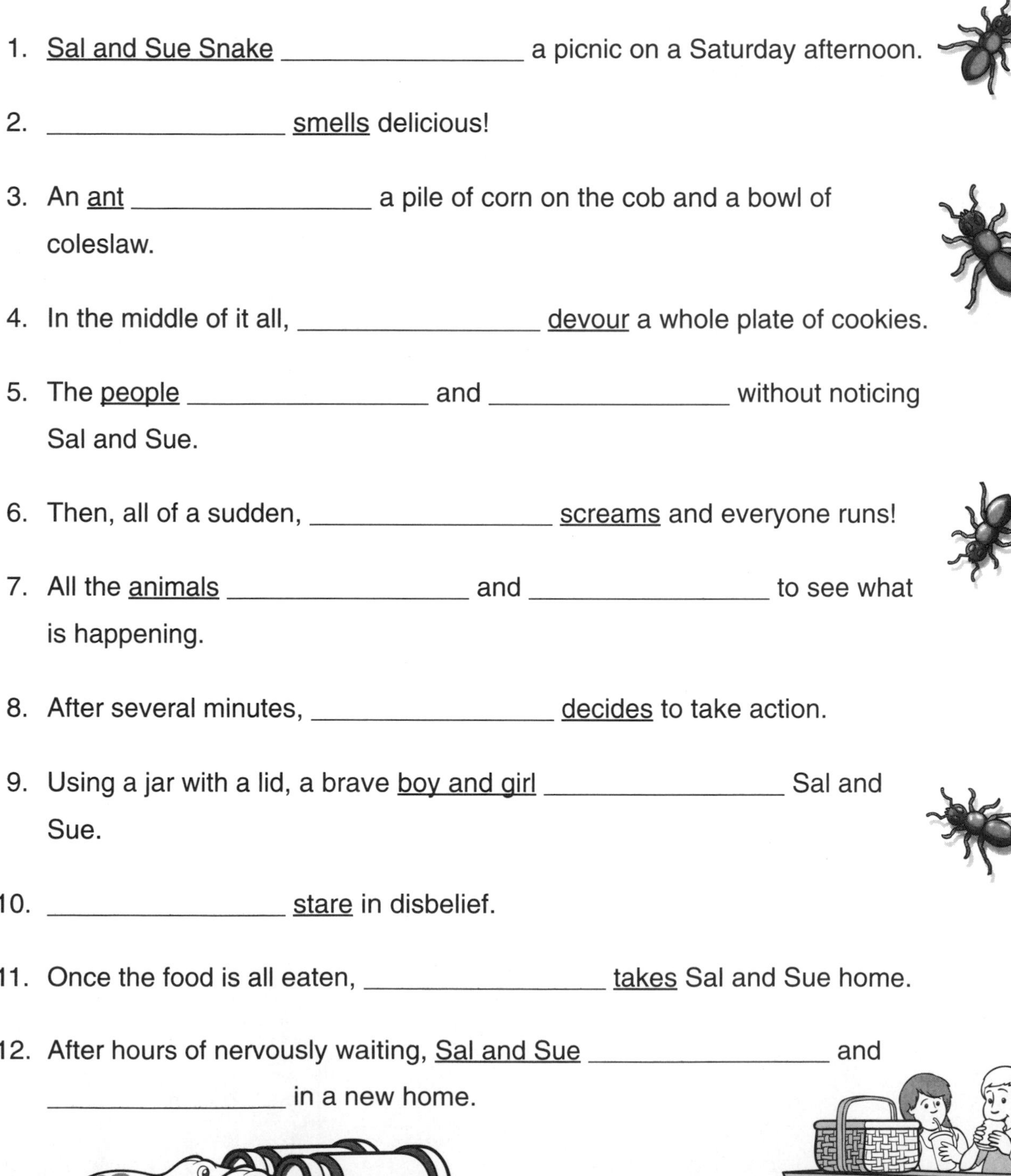

1. Sal and Sue Snake ________________ a picnic on a Saturday afternoon.
2. ________________ smells delicious!
3. An ant ________________ a pile of corn on the cob and a bowl of coleslaw.
4. In the middle of it all, ________________ devour a whole plate of cookies.
5. The people ________________ and ________________ without noticing Sal and Sue.
6. Then, all of a sudden, ________________ screams and everyone runs!
7. All the animals ________________ and ________________ to see what is happening.
8. After several minutes, ________________ decides to take action.
9. Using a jar with a lid, a brave boy and girl ________________ Sal and Sue.
10. ________________ stare in disbelief.
11. Once the food is all eaten, ________________ takes Sal and Sue home.
12. After hours of nervously waiting, Sal and Sue ________________ and ________________ in a new home.

Name

Unpredictable Verbs

1. Cut apart the cards below.
2. Glue the three heading cards to another sheet of paper as shown.
3. Glue the verb cards under the corresponding headings.
4. On a sheet of notebook paper, write three sentences. In the first sentence, use a verb from the first section. In the second sentence, use a verb from the second section. In the third sentence, use a verb from the third section.

Present Now I...	Past Yesterday I...	Past Participle I have/had _____ many times before...

begin	swum	choose	drew	bitten
saw	known	come	chosen	begun
swam	bite	break	did	come
drawn	know	bit	do	came
began	broken	swim	seen	broke
chose	done	draw	knew	see

Stake Your Claim!

(Pages 30 and 31)

Directions for two players:

1. Cut off the answer key on your other page and turn it facedown. Choose a different-colored pencil than your partner.
2. Cut apart the cards below. Stack them facedown next to the gameboard.
3. In turn, draw a card. Read aloud its verb and identify its form: past, present, or past participle.
4. Have your partner check your answer with the key. If you are correct, color a footprint on your game path. If you are incorrect, your turn is over.
5. The first player to color all the footprints on his game path wins.

blow	leave	hide	write	blew	left
hid	wrote	blown	left	hidden or hid	written
bring	lose	grow	wear	brought	lost
grew	wore	brought	lost	grown	worn
drink	ride	give	take	drank	rode
gave	took	drunk	ridden	given	taken
eat	ring	freeze	speak	ate	rang
froze	spoke	eaten	rung	frozen	spoken
forget	shake	forgot	shook	forgotten or forgot	shaken

Stake Your Claim!

Answer Key

Present	Past	Past Participle	Present	Past	Past Participle
blow	blew	blown	leave	left	left
bring	brought	brought	lose	lost	lost
drink	drank	drunk	ride	rode	ridden
eat	ate	eaten	ring	rang	rung
forget	forgot	forgotten or forgot	shake	shook	shaken
freeze	froze	frozen	speak	spoke	spoken
give	gave	given	take	took	taken
grow	grew	grown	wear	wore	worn
hide	hid	hidden or hid	write	wrote	written

Note to the teacher: Use with "Stake Your Claim!" on page 30.

Batter Up!

Write the correct verb form.

1. Most fans ___ ___ [ ] for their tickets in advance. (pay (present))
2. Some fans had ___ ___ ___ [ ] signs to cheer on the team. (make (past participle))
3. That singer has ___ ___ [ ] ___ the national anthem at the ballpark many times. (sing (past participle))
4. The pitcher ___ ___ ___ [ ] ___ the ball over the plate as fast as he could. (throw (past))
5. The batter [ ] ___ ___ ___ ___ the bat hard. (swing (past))
6. When the bat ___ ___ ___ the ball, the ball [ ] ___ ___ ___ high into the air. (meet (past); fly (past))
7. The center fielder ___ ___ [ ] ___ for the ball. (dive (past))
8. Just before the outfielder reached the ball, he suddenly ___ [ ] ___ ___ to the ground. (fall (past))
9. Because the ball was not ___ [ ] ___ ___ ___ ___, the runner ___ ___ ___ to second base. (catch (past participle); run (past))
10. The next batter ___ [ ] ___ ___ to the plate. (come (past))
11. The pitcher had never ___ ___ [ ] ___ ___ ___ out that player before. (strike (past participle))
12. His turn at bat ___ ___ ___ [ ] to a full count before he ___ ___ ___ ___ the ball over the fence for a home run. (go (past); send (past))

Why is a baseball park so cool?

To answer the question, write the boxed letter of each word from above on its matching numbered line below.

Because there's a ___ ___ ___ in ___ ___ ___ ___ ___ ___ ___ ___ ___!

(6 9 3 — 2 7 4 11 1 — 5 8 10 12)

Road Signs

(Pages 33 and 34)

1. Cut out the sentence strips below.
2. Match the strips to form six sensible compound sentences.
3. Glue the strips in the boxes on your other page. Add a capital letter and a period to each sentence.

in July, my family took a vacation	flashing lights told us that a train was coming
we saw traffic signs everywhere we went	one sign we saw had eight sides
my dad wanted to cross the tracks at a railroad crossing	I wanted Dad to drive faster
Dad could have turned left at one intersection	he could have gone straight until he came to a stop sign
he could turn the van around in a parking lot	it was red with white letters
he had to obey the speed limit signs	the sign told Dad he could make a U-turn to go back the way we came

Name

Road Signs

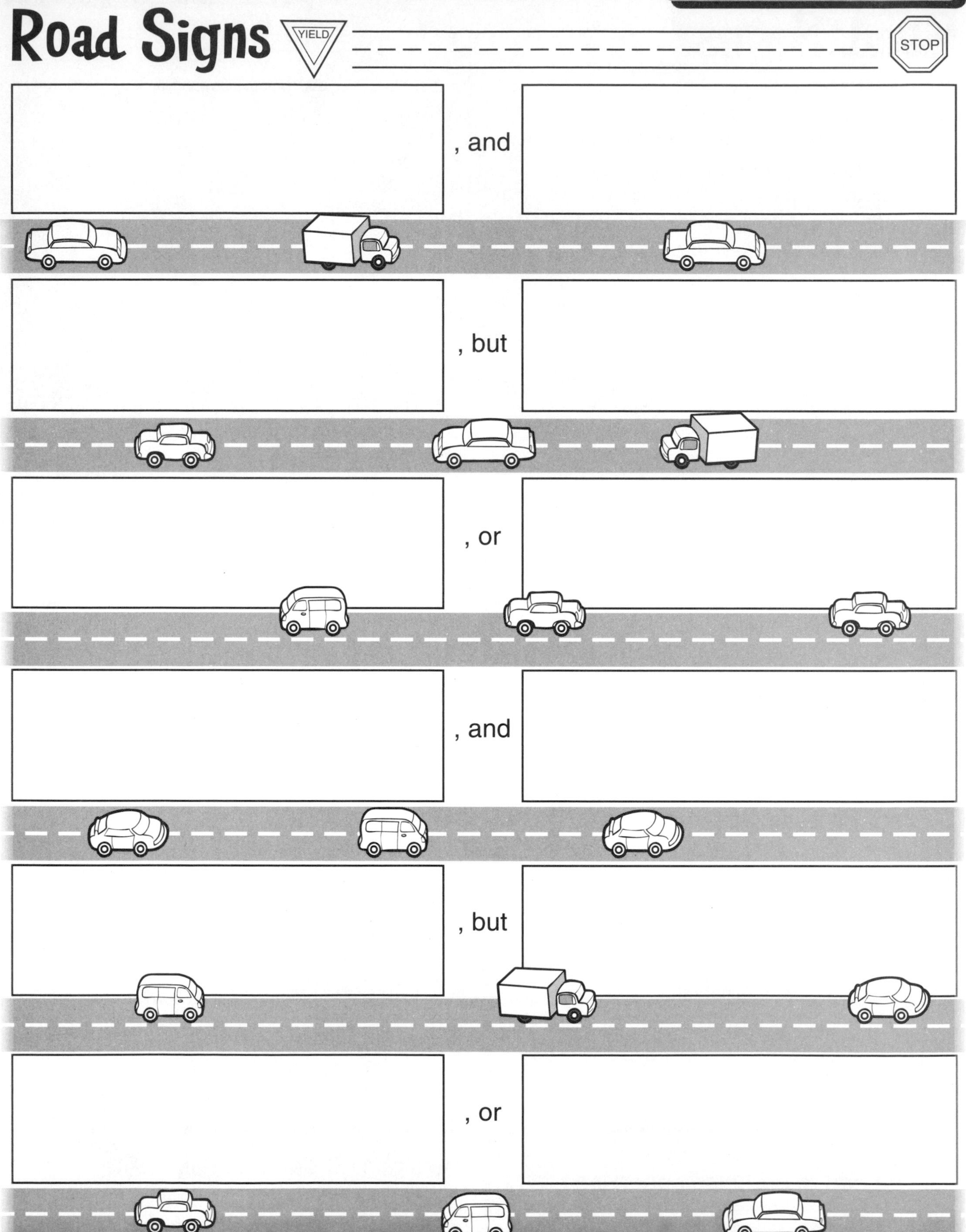

 Note to the teacher: Use with "Road Signs" on page 33.

Name

Time to Play!

Use *and, or,* or *but* to join each pair of sentences according to the code. Use correct punctuation.

A Brian asked Trevor to come over and play video games.
B Brian had a new game that was hard to play.
C Trevor loves to play video games.
D Brian prefers sports games.
E Brian offered Trevor a snack.
F Brian said they could eat chips and popcorn.
G Brian took some cookies.
H Brian munched on his snack while he played.

1 Trevor likes all kinds of games.
2 He knew Trevor could figure it out.
3 Trevor said he would like something crunchy.
4 Trevor said he would.
5 They could eat cookies his mom had baked.
6 Trevor ate his snack after the game.
7 He plays all of them well.
8 He did not take any popcorn or chips.

Code

A 4 ______________________________

B 2 ______________________________

C 7 ______________________________

D 1 ______________________________

E 3 ______________________________

F 5 ______________________________

G 8 ______________________________

H 6 ______________________________

Name

What a Storm!

1. Use a pencil and a paper clip to spin each spinner.
2. On notebook paper, write a compound sentence that includes each word or phrase spun. Use *and, or,* or *but* to join the two sentences.
3. Continue spinning until you have written ten compound sentences and used *and, or,* and *but* at least three times each.

A

sharp lightning

dark clouds

heavy showers

the thunderstorm

loud thunder

the lights in our house

Name

Race to the Finish!

1. Cut out the cards below.
2. Create eight complex sentences by matching each numbered card to its correct lettered card.
3. Glue the matching pairs of cards to another sheet of paper. Then rewrite each sentence on notebook paper using the correct punctuation and capitalization.

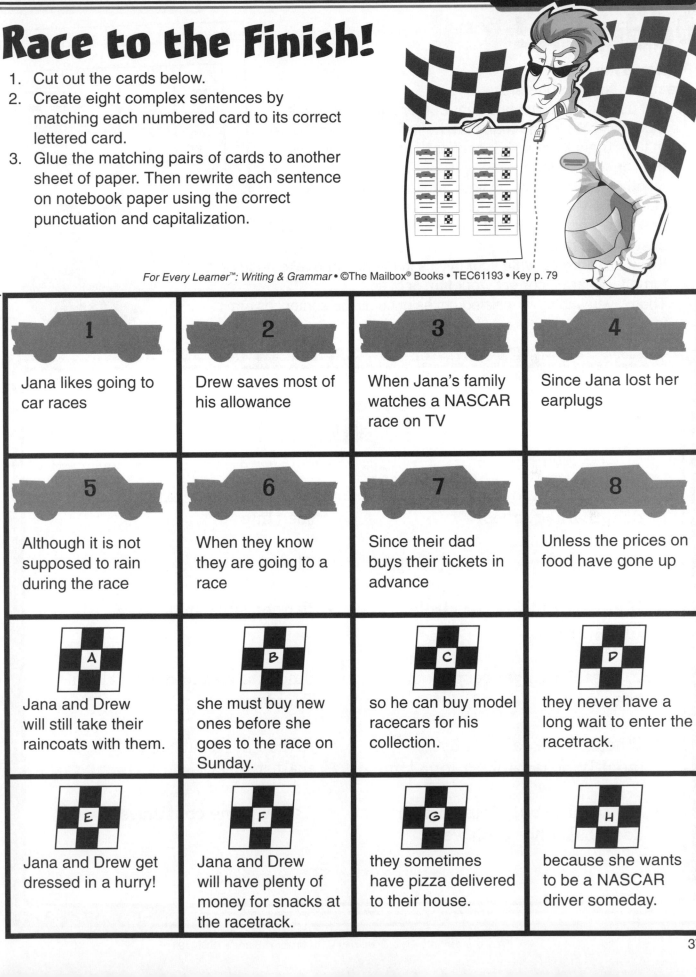

1 Jana likes going to car races	2 Drew saves most of his allowance	3 When Jana's family watches a NASCAR race on TV	4 Since Jana lost her earplugs
5 Although it is not supposed to rain during the race	6 When they know they are going to a race	7 Since their dad buys their tickets in advance	8 Unless the prices on food have gone up
 A Jana and Drew will still take their raincoats with them.	 B she must buy new ones before she goes to the race on Sunday.	 C so he can buy model racecars for his collection.	 D they never have a long wait to enter the racetrack.
 E Jana and Drew get dressed in a hurry!	 F Jana and Drew will have plenty of money for snacks at the racetrack.	 G they sometimes have pizza delivered to their house.	 H because she wants to be a NASCAR driver someday.

Dodge It!

(Pages 38 and 39)

Directions for two players:

1. Cut out the answer key on your other page and turn it facedown. Write your name at the top of the gameboard.
2. In turn, draw a vertical or horizontal line to connect two dots on the gameboard.
3. If you complete a box on your turn, form a complex sentence by combining a clause from below with the one enclosed in the box. Have your partner check your answer with the key.
4. If you are correct, write your initials in the box and take another turn. If you are incorrect, your turn is over.
5. The player with more initialed boxes once all the sentences are formed wins.

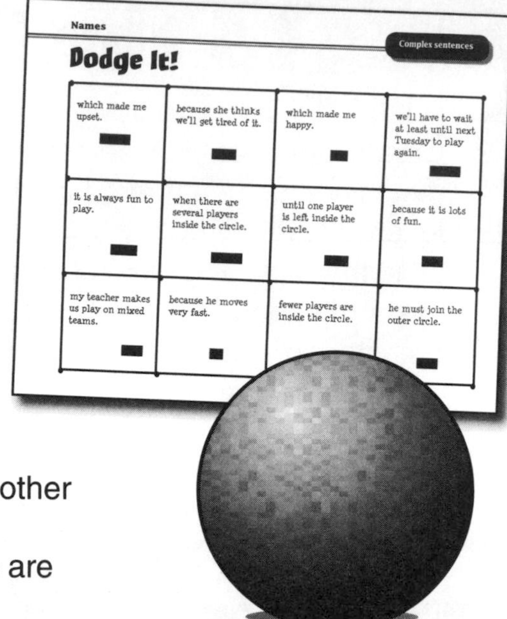

Clauses

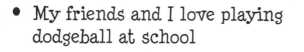

- My friends and I love playing dodgeball at school
- Tanner's throw hit me too hard,
- If a player inside the circle gets hit by the ball,
- It is easier to get people out of the game
- Whether the game is over quickly or lasts for a long time,
- My teacher only lets us play dodgeball once each week
- Brent wins the game most of the time
- The game continues
- Tanner later apologized,
- Since we played dodgeball on Tuesdays,
- Although I'd rather play boys against girls,
- As the game continues,

Names

Dodge It!

which made me upset.

because she thinks we'll get tired of it.

which made me happy.

we'll have to wait at least until next Tuesday to play again.

it is always fun to play.

when there are several players inside the circle.

until one player is left inside the circle.

because it is lots of fun.

my teacher makes us play on mixed teams.

because he moves very fast.

fewer players are inside the circle.

he must join the outer circle.

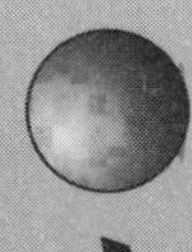

Answer Key for "Dodge It!"

- My friends and I love playing dodgeball at school because it is lots of fun.
- Tanner's throw hit me too hard, which made me upset.
- It is easier to get people out of the game when there are several players inside the circle.
- The game continues until one player is left inside the circle.
- My teacher only lets us play dodgeball once each week because she thinks we'll get tired of it.
- If a player inside the circle gets hit by the ball, he must join the outer circle.
- Brent wins the game most of the time because he moves very fast.
- Tanner later apologized, which made me happy.
- Since we played dodgeball on Tuesdays, we'll have to wait at least until next Tuesday to play again.
- Whether the game is over quickly or lasts for a long time, it is always fun to play.
- Although I'd rather play boys against girls, my teacher makes us play on mixed teams.
- As the game continues, fewer players are inside the circle.

Note to the teacher: Use with "Dodge It!" on page 38.

Name

The Doctor Is In!

Find a related sentence in each of the three columns.
Draw lines to match the three sentences.
Use a word from the word bank to rewrite the three sentences as one complex sentence.
Continue until you have written five new sentences on the lines below.

Word Bank

after	that
although	though
as	till
as if	unless
because	until
before	when
for	whenever
if	where
once	whereas
since	wherever
so	whether
so that	while
than	

1. Dr. Fisher is my doctor.
2. I started feeling ill.
3. My throat was sore.
4. Dr. Fisher always wears a white coat.
5. I have a little sister.
6. I started feeling ill yesterday.
7. My little sister wants to be like Dr. Fisher.
8. I go to Dr. Fisher's office to get a checkup.
9. Dr. Fisher always wears a stethoscope.
10. My throat was scratchy.
11. I could hardly swallow.
12. My doctor gives me the shots I need.
13. Dr. Fisher helps people.
14. I went to see Dr. Fisher yesterday.
15. Dr. Fisher always wears the same things.

1. ______________________________

____

2. ______________________________

____

3. ______________________________

____

4. ______________________________

____

5. ______________________________

____

Whirling Winds

(Pages 41 and 42)

1. Cut apart the sentence strips below.
2. Match each detail strip to a main idea on your other page.
3. Glue the strips in place on your other page.
4. On notebook paper, write a three-paragraph report on tornadoes. Use the topic sentences and supporting details from your other page.

- If you can't get inside, lie flat and cover your head.
- Winds are very destructive.
- Winds swirl at very high speeds.
- Tornadoes are studied in labs and outdoors.
- Park and get out of a car.
- Some scientists film real tornadoes.
- Go to the lowest floor of a building.
- Stay away from windows.
- Scientists hope to learn why tornadoes form.
- Powerful tornadoes can lift cows and cars off the ground.
- Get out of a mobile home.
- Tornadoes can last from a few minutes to over an hour.

Name

Organizing details

Whirling Winds

It's a twister, Bertha! Lie flat!

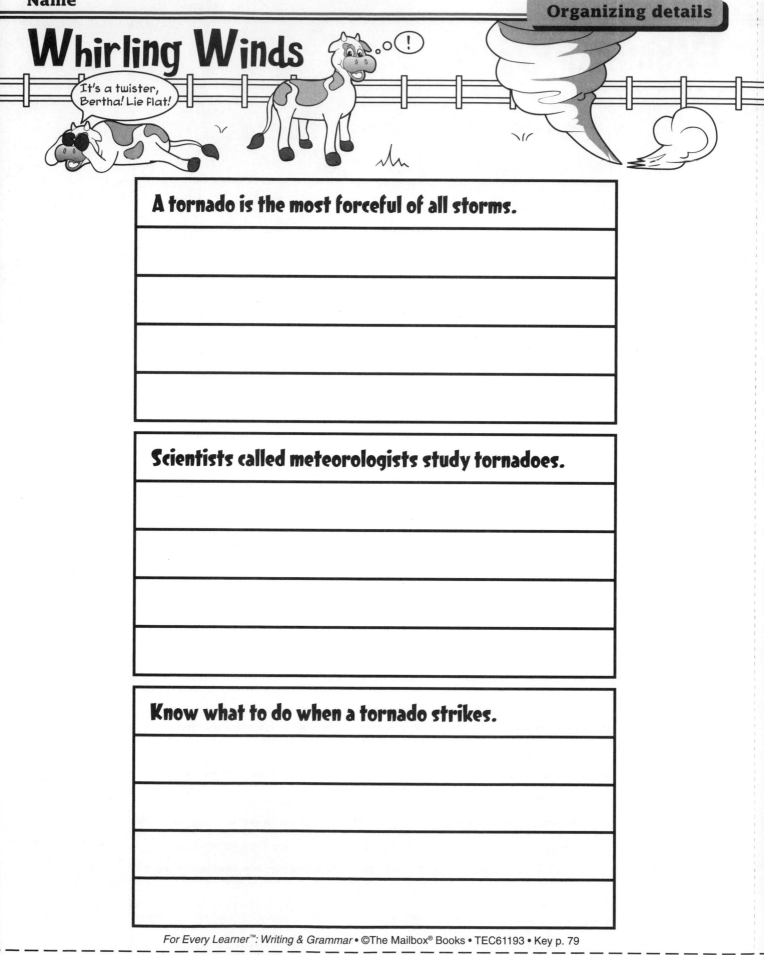

A tornado is the most forceful of all storms.

Scientists called meteorologists study tornadoes.

Know what to do when a tornado strikes.

 Note to the teacher: Use with "Whirling Winds" on page 41.

Name

Coyotes in the News

Color the circles to match each detail to a topic sentence.
Use the color code.

Code

blue = Coyotes are being spotted in unusual places.
green = Coyotes look a lot like dogs, but there are differences.
red = If you see a coyote, remember these things.

(1) Never give a coyote food.

(2) They are in backyards across the country.

(3) Their snouts are slender like those of foxes.

(4) Move slowly toward people or shelter.

(5) Their eyes are golden yellow.

(6) A coyote was seen on a train in Portland, Oregon.

(7) They are often afraid of people.

(8) They trot across city streets.

(9) Wave your arms and make lots of noise.

(10) People in New York have seen them in Central Park.

(11) They have bushy tails that hang down.

(12) Never run away because the coyote may chase you.

On another sheet of paper, write a three-paragraph report on coyotes. Use the topic sentences and supporting details from above.

Name

A Bug-Eating Plant

1. Cut apart the sentence strips below and sort them into three categories.
2. Fold another sheet of paper into three sections.
3. At the top of each section, write a topic sentence for each category.
4. Glue each group of strips under the matching topic sentence.
5. On notebook paper, write a three-paragraph report on the Venus flytrap. Use the topic sentences and supporting details from your categories.

It takes five to 12 days for a plant to digest a bug.
Dead leaves fall off the plant and new ones grow.
A Venus flytrap is about one foot tall.
The leaf closes even tighter around the bug.
It has white flowers and odd-shaped leaves.
The leaf snaps shut and the bug is trapped.
The leaf reopens when the plant is finished eating.
Each leaf has two halves that are joined.
A bug lands on a leaf and makes contact with trigger hairs.
The bug wiggles as it tries to get away.
Each leaf half has stiff hairs that work like triggers.
Each leaf can eat three meals before it dies.

Name

Tarantula Tidbits

Cut apart the strips below.
Select the eight strips with the most important details about tarantulas.
Glue the strips to the spider's legs.
Use the details to write a paragraph about tarantulas on another sheet of paper.

Tarantulas, the World's Largest Spiders

like warm climates	*sometimes appear in movies*	*live in South America and the southwestern United States*
can live as long as 20 years	*sometimes dig underground burrows for their nests*	*are well liked*
sometimes live in trees	*are not usually very poisonous*	*cannot see very well*
have an Italian folk dance named after them	*sometimes eat small rodents and reptiles*	*have a four-syllable name*

Fantastic Frog Facts

1. Cut out the puzzle pieces.
2. Select the pieces that have the most important information about frogs.
3. Put the pieces together to form a frog shape.
4. Glue your frog puzzle to the bottom of another sheet of paper.
5. Use the details to write a paragraph about frogs in the space above your puzzle.

no tail

bulging eyes

liked by kids

strong hind legs

no neck

famous one named Kermit

length varies from a half inch to almost a foot

catches food by quickly flicking out its sticky tongue

can live in trees

amphibian that spends part of its life in water and part on land

found everywhere except Antarctica

eaten by some people

can be brown, green, or brightly colored

can live underground

breathes through its lungs and skin as an adult

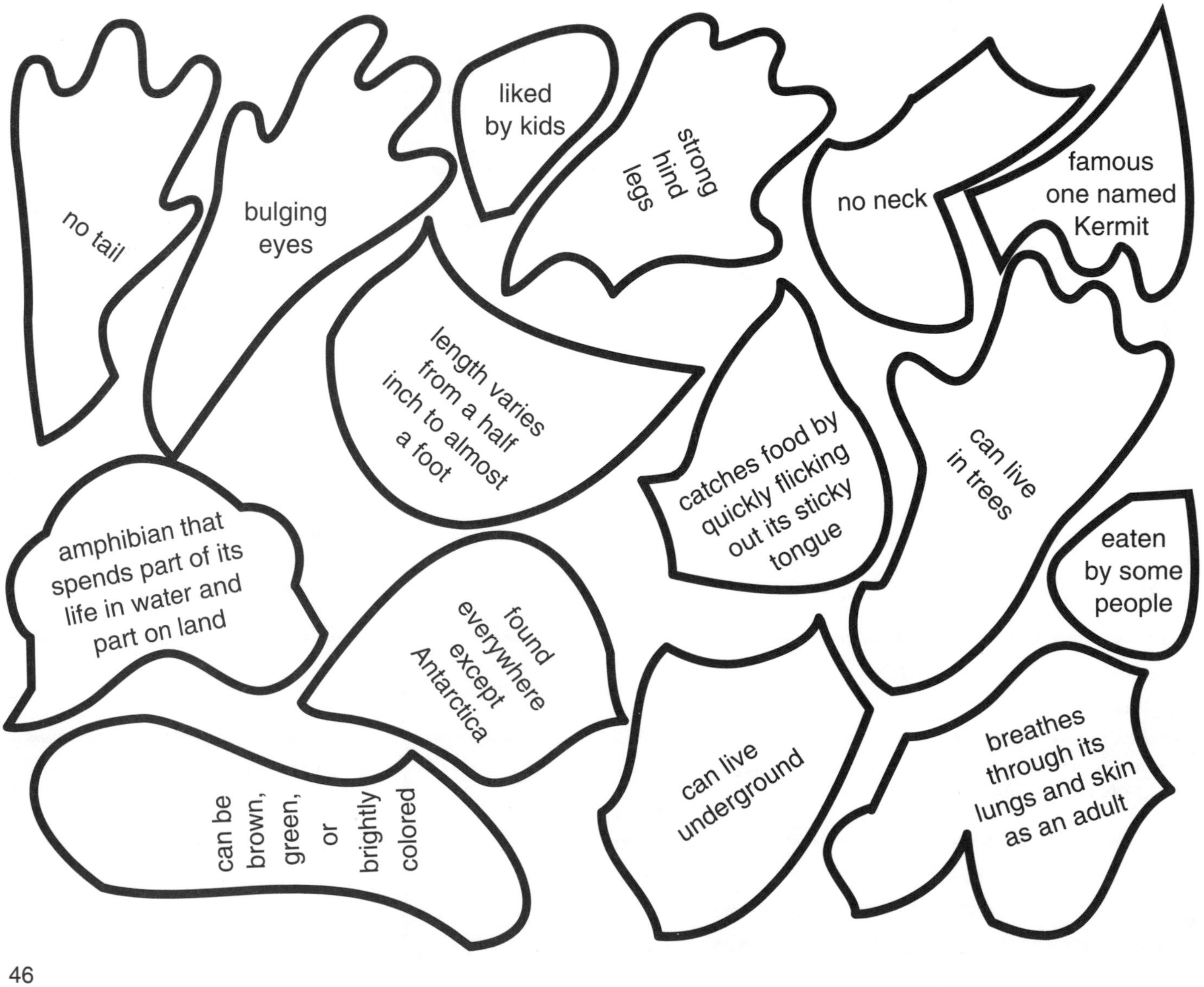

Wanted!

(Pages 47 and 48)

1. Read the poster on your other page. Notice that some important details are missing.
2. Cut out the cards below.
3. Select ten cards that provide more details about the information on the poster.
4. Use a ^ with the card's number to mark on your other page where you will insert that detail.
5. Rewrite each poster section, adding the selected details, on another sheet of paper.

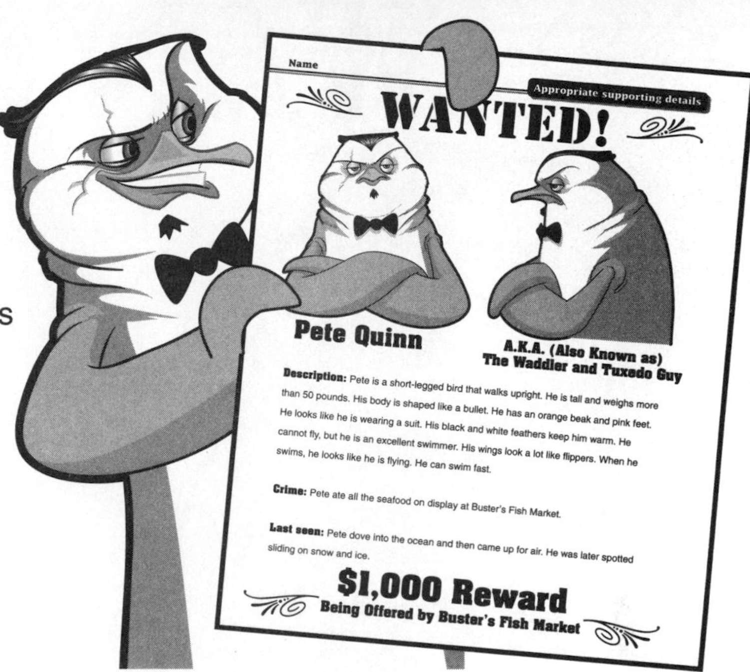

Name

Appropriate supporting details

WANTED!

Pete Quinn

A.K.A. (Also Known as) The Waddler and Tuxedo Guy

Description: Pete is a short-legged bird that walks upright. He is tall and weighs more than 50 pounds. His body is shaped like a bullet. He has an orange beak and pink feet. He looks like he is wearing a suit. His black and white feathers keep him warm. He cannot fly, but he is an excellent swimmer. His wings look a lot like flippers. When he swims, he looks like he is flying. He can swim fast.

Crime: Pete ate all the seafood on display at Buster's Fish Market.

Last seen: Pete dove into the ocean and then came up for air. He was later spotted sliding on snow and ice.

$1,000 Reward

Being Offered by Buster's Fish Market

slides on his belly over snow and ice

looks like he is wearing a black tuxedo because his front feathers are white like the bibbed part of a tuxedo shirt

likes to eat fish, crabs, shrimps, and squid

has short, thick feathers that are waterproof

spends time on ice and snow

is about four feet tall

weighs about 85 pounds

swims about eight miles per hour

is funny to look at

swims in the cold water far south of the equator near Antarctica

has been in a movie

leaps out of the water every minute or so for air

has a stuffed animal named after him

spends time in the water

walks on two legs like a person

Name

Appropriate supporting details

WANTED!

A.K.A. (Also Known as) The Waddler and Tuxedo Guy

Description: Pete is a short-legged bird that walks upright. He is tall and weighs more than 50 pounds. His body is shaped like a bullet. He has an orange beak and pink feet. He looks like he is wearing a suit. His black and white feathers keep him warm. He cannot fly, but he is an excellent swimmer. His wings look a lot like flippers. When he swims, he looks like he is flying. He can swim fast.

Crime: Pete ate all the seafood on display at Buster's Fish Market.

Last seen: Pete dove into the ocean and then came up for air. He was later spotted sliding on snow and ice.

$1,000 Reward

Being Offered by Buster's Fish Market

Note to the teacher: Use with "Wanted!" on page 47.

It's "A-maize-ing"!

(Pages 49 and 50)

Directions for two players:

1. Cut out the word bank and answer key below. Place the answer key facedown. Choose a colored pencil that is a different color from your partner's.
2. In turn, draw a horizontal or diagonal line to connect two dots on your other page.
3. When you draw a line that completes a triangle, replace the next available underlined word, phrase, or sentence with a more specific word, phrase, or sentence from the word bank.
4. Have your partner use the key to check your answer. If you are correct, color the triangle and take another turn. If you are incorrect, your turn is over.
5. The player who colors more triangles wins.

WORD BANK

BRILLIANT
CONTENT
CONSTRUCT
IMMENSE
ONCE IN A WHILE,
FASCINATING
GALLOP
GRUNT AND SQUEAL
CHUCKLE
THE FARMERS ARE BAFFLED.
LAID EYES ON
MONITOR
DESIGNATED AS
MAINTAIN
ORDERLY
REMARKED

Answer Key

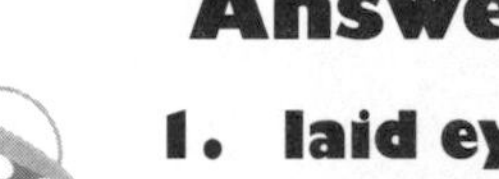
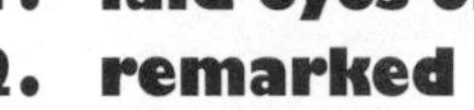

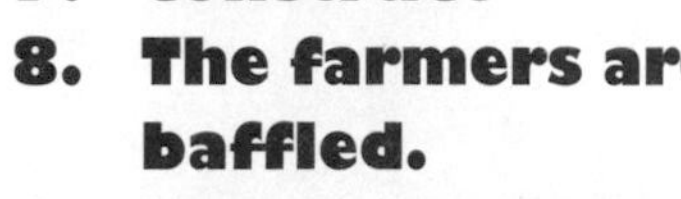
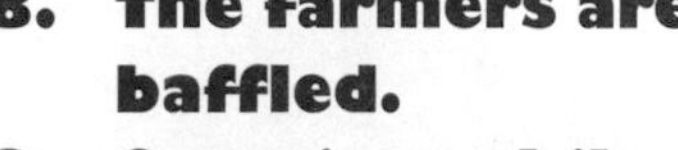

1. **laid eyes on**
2. **remarked**
3. **chuckle**
4. **monitor**
5. **orderly**
6. **designated as**
7. **construct**
8. **The farmers are baffled.**
9. **Once in a while,**
10. **immense**
11. **fascinating**
12. **brilliant**
13. **maintain**
14. **content**
15. **grunt and squeal**
16. **gallop**

It's "A-maize-ing"!

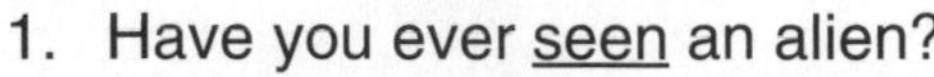

1. Have you ever seen an alien?

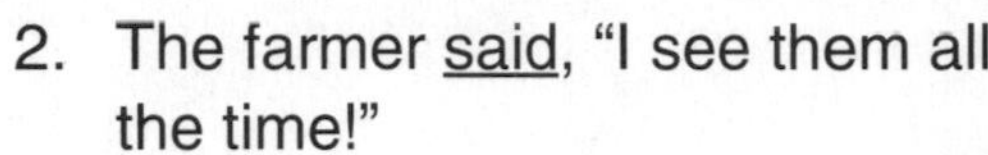

2. The farmer said, "I see them all the time!"
3. Some people laugh at the thought of aliens.
4. I like to watch the sky for UFOs.
5. Sometimes there are tidy designs in the cornfields.
6. The designs are sometimes called crop circles.
7. Maybe UFOs make the designs.
8. No one knows.
9. Sometimes new crop circles appear.
10. The designs can be big.
11. Many of the designs are interesting.
12. Even smart scientists don't know the answers.
13. Farmers keep doing their daily chores.
14. The animals are healthy and happy.
15. The pigs still make funny noises.
16. The horses still run in open fields.

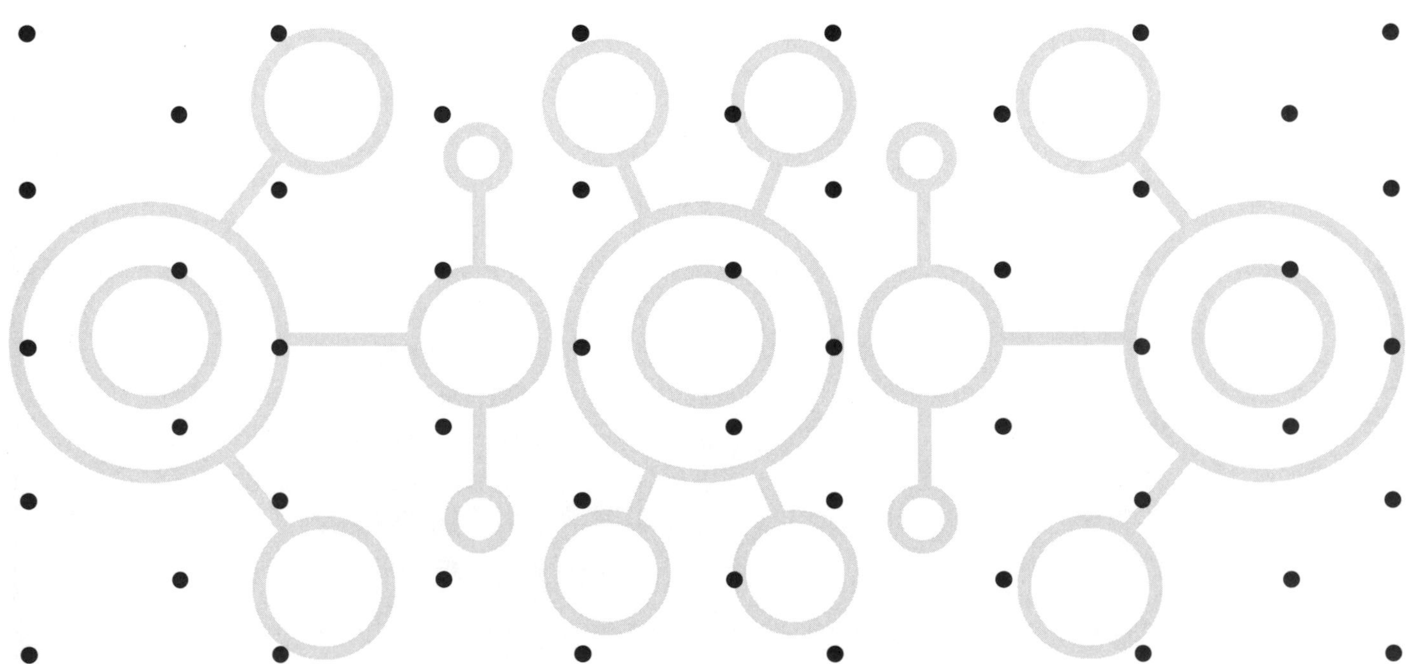

 Note to the teacher: Use with "It's 'A-maize-ing'!" on page 49.

Name

The Big Squeeze

1. Cut apart the sentence strips.
2. In sentence 1, cut out the two overused words.
3. Glue the sentence to a sheet of construction paper, leaving a space where each overused word was removed.
4. Use a thesaurus to help you write in the space a new word that makes the sentence better.
5. Repeat Steps 2–4 with each remaining sentence.

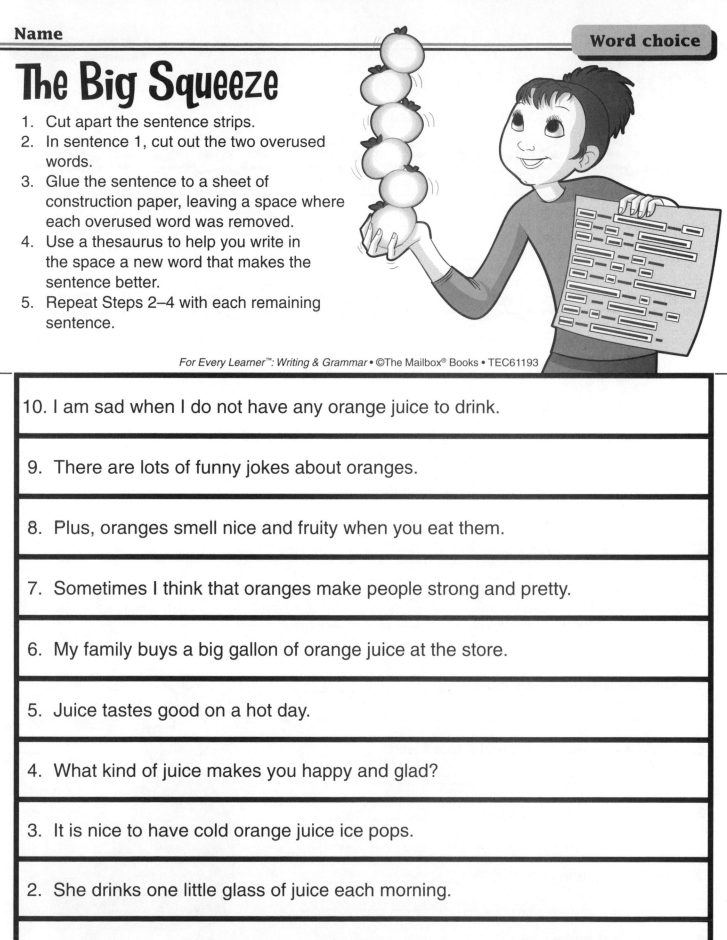

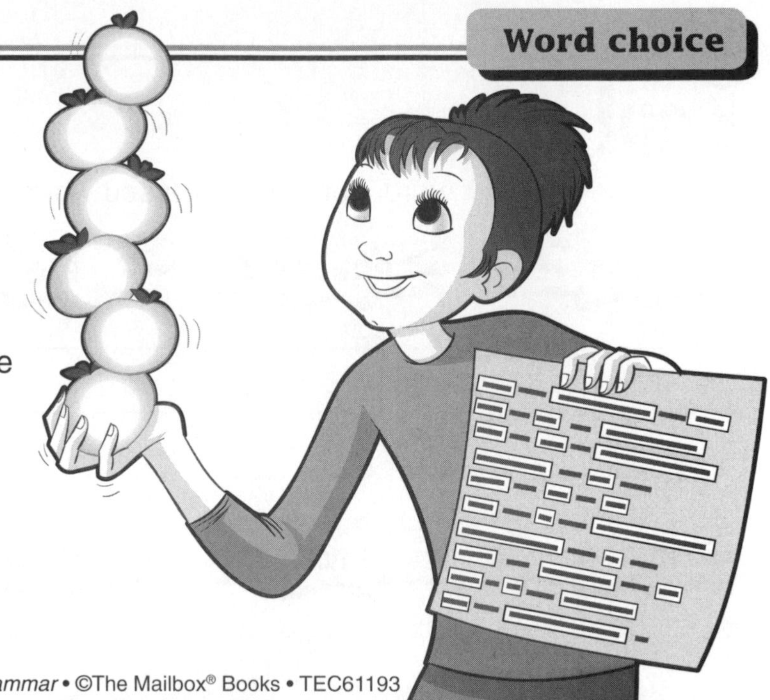

10. I am sad when I do not have any orange juice to drink.

9. There are lots of funny jokes about oranges.

8. Plus, oranges smell nice and fruity when you eat them.

7. Sometimes I think that oranges make people strong and pretty.

6. My family buys a big gallon of orange juice at the store.

5. Juice tastes good on a hot day.

4. What kind of juice makes you happy and glad?

3. It is nice to have cold orange juice ice pops.

2. She drinks one little glass of juice each morning.

1. Felicia said, “I like orange juice because it is good and refreshing!”

Name

Zap!

Write three stronger words for each overused word.

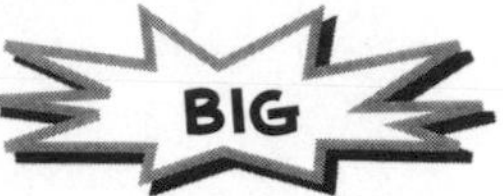

Read each sentence. Draw a lightning bolt over each overused word.
Rewrite each sentence using more interesting words.

1. "I am happy that I won the lottery," said Kevin. ______________________________

2. My little dog likes fetching. ______________________________

3. It is fun to watch the stars. ______________________________

4. Kevin said that he likes movies. ______________________________

5. Kayla is a good student and a nice friend. ______________________________

6. The big lion ran after its prey. ______________________________

7. This video game is neat. ______________________________

8. She looked pretty. ______________________________

Name

A Wild Adventure

1. Cut out the cards and strips below.
2. Glue the paragraph cards in order to the left side of another sheet of paper.
3. Read the first paragraph and each sentence on the two matching strips. Glue the better summary next to paragraph 1.
4. Repeat Step 3 with each remaining paragraph.

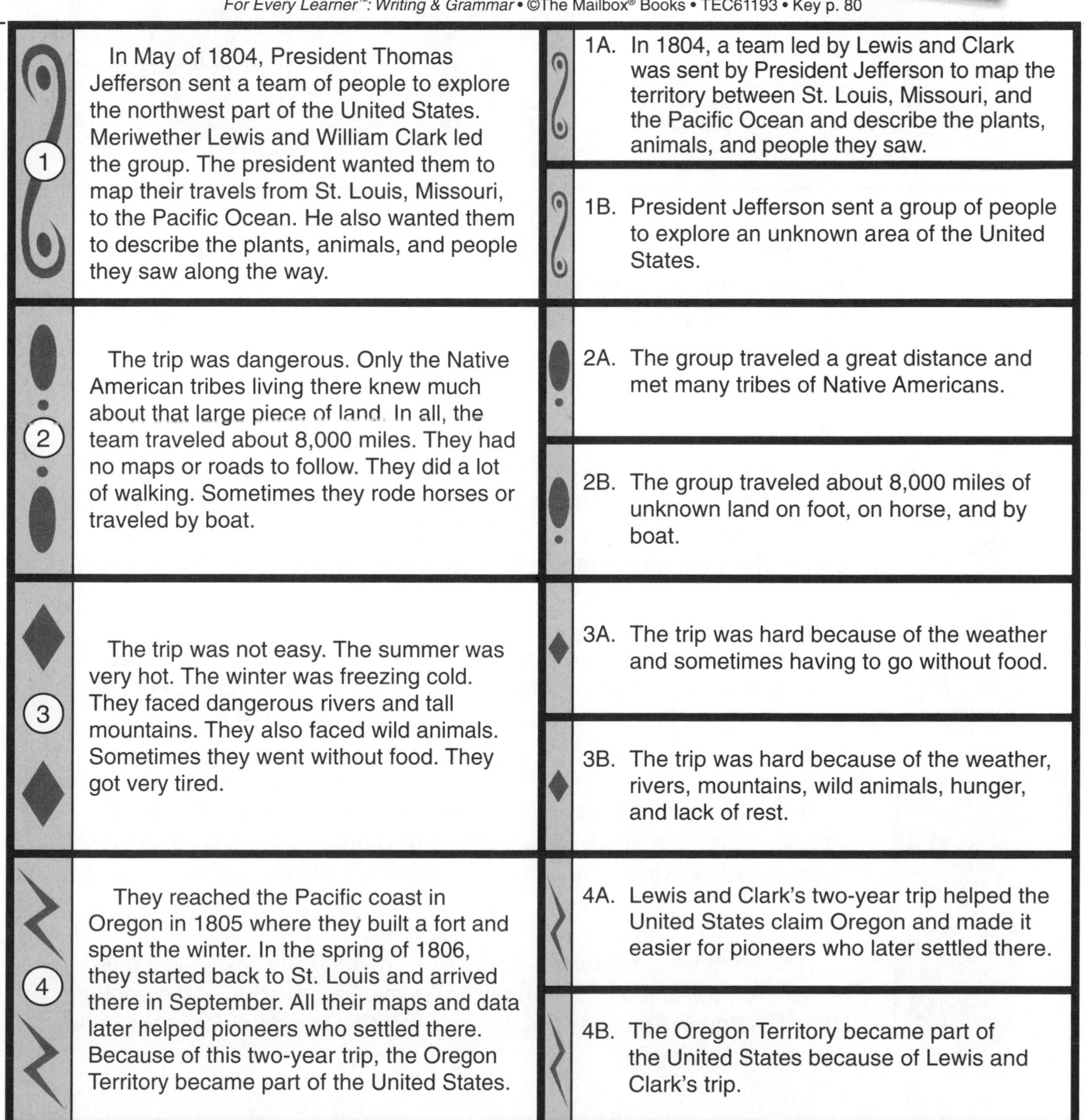

1 In May of 1804, President Thomas Jefferson sent a team of people to explore the northwest part of the United States. Meriwether Lewis and William Clark led the group. The president wanted them to map their travels from St. Louis, Missouri, to the Pacific Ocean. He also wanted them to describe the plants, animals, and people they saw along the way.	1A. In 1804, a team led by Lewis and Clark was sent by President Jefferson to map the territory between St. Louis, Missouri, and the Pacific Ocean and describe the plants, animals, and people they saw. 1B. President Jefferson sent a group of people to explore an unknown area of the United States.
2 The trip was dangerous. Only the Native American tribes living there knew much about that large piece of land. In all, the team traveled about 8,000 miles. They had no maps or roads to follow. They did a lot of walking. Sometimes they rode horses or traveled by boat.	2A. The group traveled a great distance and met many tribes of Native Americans. 2B. The group traveled about 8,000 miles of unknown land on foot, on horse, and by boat.
3 The trip was not easy. The summer was very hot. The winter was freezing cold. They faced dangerous rivers and tall mountains. They also faced wild animals. Sometimes they went without food. They got very tired.	3A. The trip was hard because of the weather and sometimes having to go without food. 3B. The trip was hard because of the weather, rivers, mountains, wild animals, hunger, and lack of rest.
4 They reached the Pacific coast in Oregon in 1805 where they built a fort and spent the winter. In the spring of 1806, they started back to St. Louis and arrived there in September. All their maps and data later helped pioneers who settled there. Because of this two-year trip, the Oregon Territory became part of the United States.	4A. Lewis and Clark's two-year trip helped the United States claim Oregon and made it easier for pioneers who later settled there. 4B. The Oregon Territory became part of the United States because of Lewis and Clark's trip.

Name

Summarizing

Tea Chests Overboard!

(Pages 54 and 55)

1. Read the first paragraph below.
2. On your other page, summarize the main idea by completing the sentence on the matching tea chest.
3. Repeat for paragraphs 2–5.

In 1767, the American colonies were controlled by Great Britain. To pay the cost of shipping items to the colonies, the British government put a tax on many things the colonists used. This angered the colonists, so they refused to pay the taxes. In 1773, the British government removed all taxes but the one on tea.

When tea ships came into Boston Harbor in 1773 with 90,000 pounds of tea, the colonists wanted them sent right back to England. They thought that if they paid the tea tax, it would lead to paying more taxes in the future. The British governor in Boston refused to send the ships back.

Many colonists were very angry. One group decided to take action. They dressed up as Native Americans and put coal dust and paint on their faces. They put feathers in their hats and marched to the harbor.

The disguised colonists boarded the three British ships. The British soldiers gave them the keys without fighting and left the ship. The men opened 342 heavy chests and dumped the tea into the harbor.

This event became known as the Boston Tea Party. It was just one of the events that led to the American Revolution and the forming of the United States of America. The colonists felt that freedom from harsh rule was worth fighting for.

Name

Tea Chests Overboard!

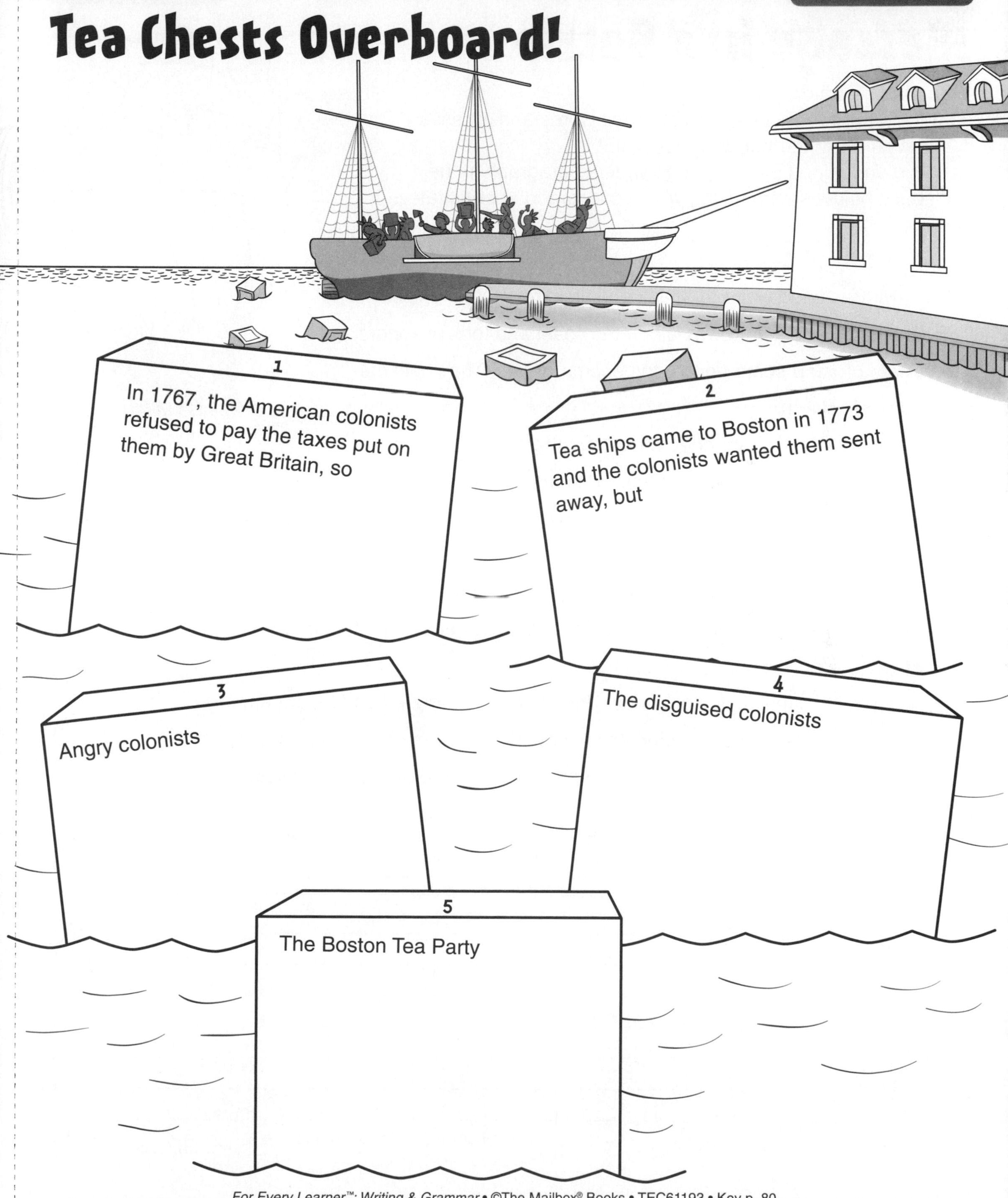
1
In 1767, the American colonists refused to pay the taxes put on them by Great Britain, so
2
Tea ships came to Boston in 1773 and the colonists wanted them sent away, but
3
Angry colonists
4
The disguised colonists
5
The Boston Tea Party

Note to the teacher: Use with "Tea Chests Overboard!" on page 54.

Name

Message in a Bottle

Read the selection below.
In each paragraph, underline important words and phrases that tell what the paragraph is about.
Use the underlined information to write a paragraph in the space below summarizing what you learned about pirates.

Pirates used ships to attack and steal from other ships. They also attacked towns along the coast and took prisoners. Pirates forced some people to become slaves. They held the rich for ransom.

Pirate attacks happened often from the 1500s through the 1700s. Most acts of piracy occurred on the Mediterranean and Caribbean Seas. A few pirates were women, but most were men. Some of the most famous pirates were Blackbeard, William Kidd, and Henry Morgan.

A life at sea was hard during these years. Honest sailors sometimes became pirates in order to make a living. Others became pirates to look for adventure and riches.

A pirate's life was full of danger. Pirates often quarreled and fought among themselves. Many pirates died when they got sick or injured or were left on an island to survive on their own. If a pirate was captured by the authorities, he could be put to death.

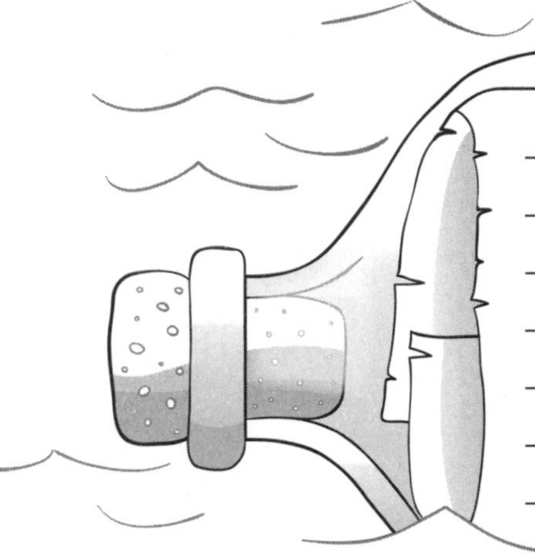

Use the back if you need more space.

What's the Story?

(Pages 57 and 58)

1. Cut out the picture cards below.
2. Choose one picture for each element on the plot line and glue it to your other page.
3. On a sheet of notebook paper, write a story using your completed plot line.

Name

What's the Story?

 Note to the teacher: Use with "What's the Story?" on page 57.

Name

Place Your Order!

Circle one event in each category of the menu. Then use the circled events to write a story on a separate sheet of paper.

Menu

For Starters
(Introduction)
A Boy on a Beach
Three Girls at a Party
A Dog and a Cat in the Kitchen
Two Frogs in a Classroom

Salads
(Rising Action)
Someone or Something Is Lost
All the Food Is Missing
Someone or Something Is in Trouble
The Power Has Gone Out

Additional Toppings
(Next Rising Action)
Someone Has Gone Crazy
Someone Doesn't Speak English
A Squirrel Enters the Story

Main Dishes
(Climax)
There Is a Struggle
All Is Quiet Until...
Something Unusual Is Seen
A Parent Shows Up

Your story is made to order. Please allow plenty of time for your story to be made.

À La Carte
(Falling Action)
A Superhero Arrives
An Agreement Is Reached
Friends Are Reunited
Someone or Something Leaves

Decadent Desserts
(Conclusion)
Everything Is Back to Normal
Nothing Is the Same Ever Again
Things Are Even Better Now
To Be Continued...

Please Come Again!

Name

Put a New Spin on It

1. Choose a topic card and cut it out.
2. Roll a die and use the code to find your challenge item. Write your challenge item on your topic card.
3. Glue the topic card to the top of a sheet of notebook paper.
4. Write a narrative about the topic. Be sure to include the challenge item in your story.

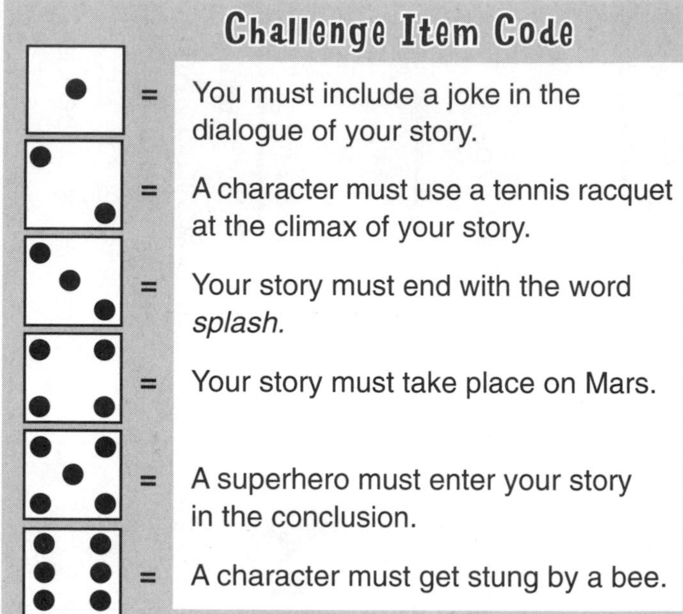

Challenge Item Code

Die		Challenge item
1	=	You must include a joke in the dialogue of your story.
2	=	A character must use a tennis racquet at the climax of your story.
3	=	Your story must end with the word *splash.*
4	=	Your story must take place on Mars.
5	=	A superhero must enter your story in the conclusion.
6	=	A character must get stung by a bee.

Imagine a group of trained fleas has escaped from a flea circus.
Challenge item: ______

Pretend you are a goofy monster hiding under a bed.
Challenge item: ______

Write a story about a rusty robot and its pet cat.
Challenge item: ______

Imagine you and your best friend go on a cruise.
Challenge item: ______

Pretend you wake one morning to a world run by giant horses.
Challenge item: ______

Write a story about winning a contest.
Challenge item: ______

Name

Delicious Details

1. Cut apart the cards below and glue them to the chart under the correct headings.
2. On notebook paper, write a paragraph describing the making, grilling, and eating of a burger. Use as many words from the chart as you can.
3. Glue this page to the back of your description.

See	Hear	Smell	Taste	Touch

Cool Clothes!

(Pages 62 and 63)

1. Add hair and facial features to the figure's head below.
2. Color and cut out on your other page the clothing items you want the figure to wear. Add more detail to each piece if you wish.
3. Cut out the figure and glue the selected cutouts to it.
4. On notebook paper, describe the figure's outfit from top to bottom or bottom to top.
5. Glue the figure to the back of your description.

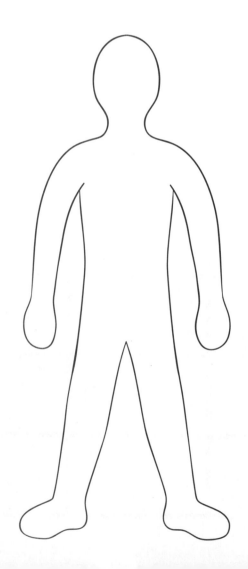

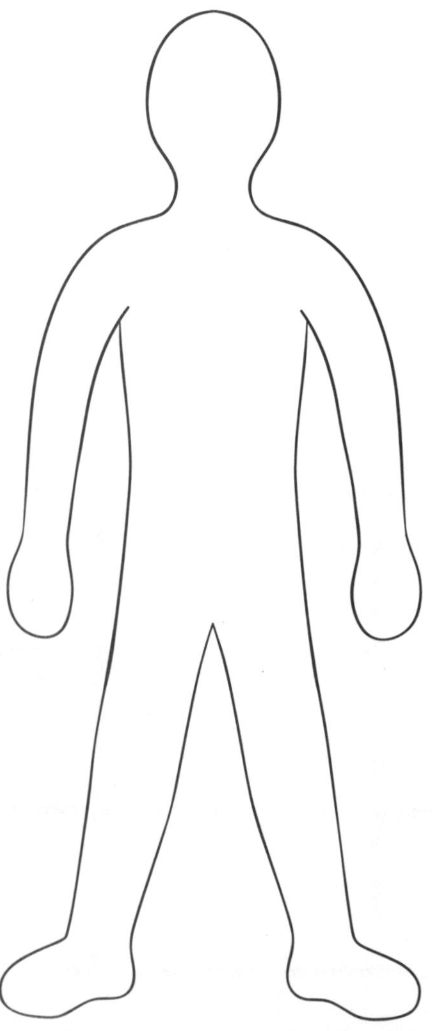

Name

Cool Clothes!

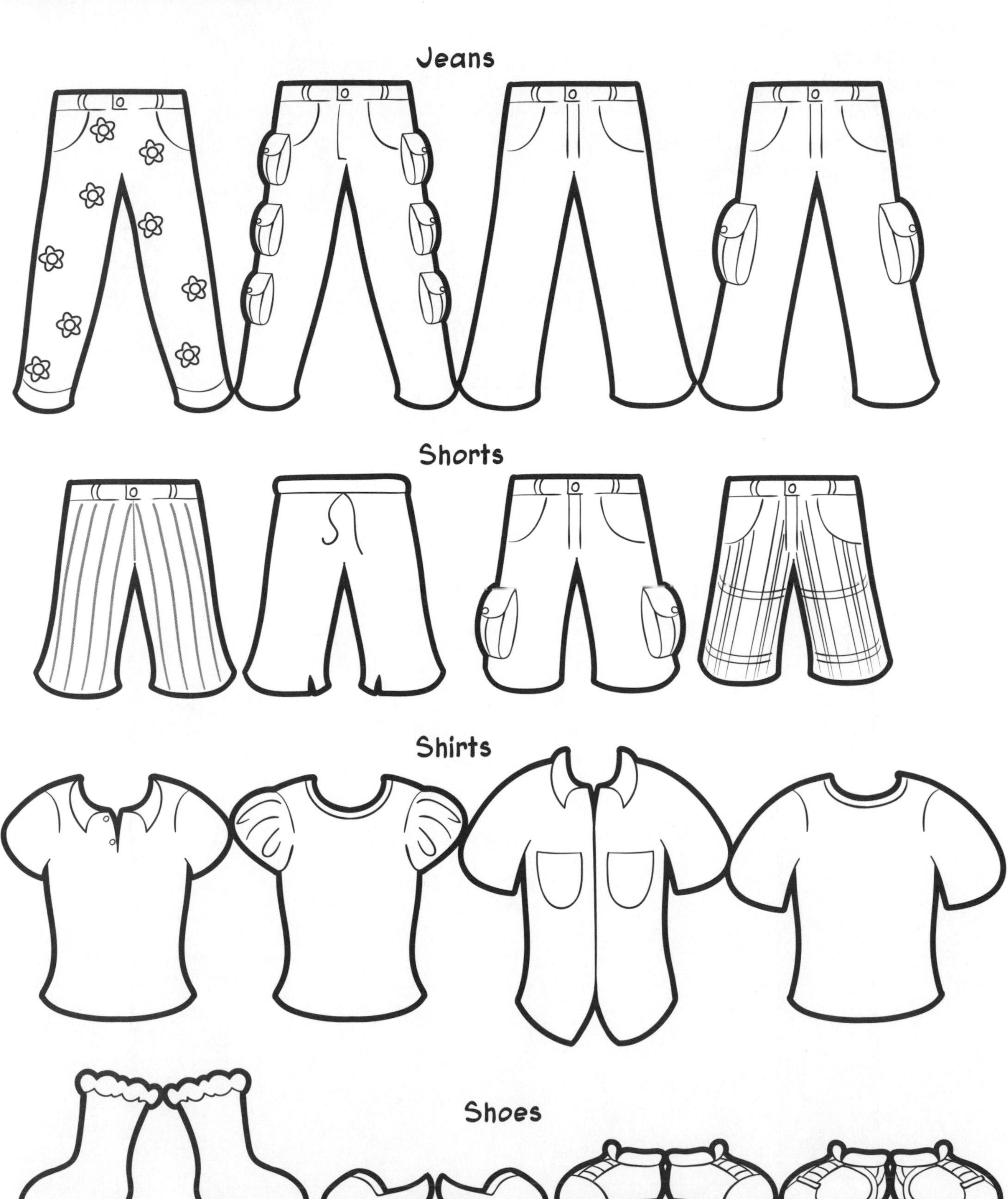

Note to the teacher: Use with "Cool Clothes!" on page 62.

Name

Take a Snapshot!

1. Cut out the frame below. Then cut out the inside of it.
2. Place the frame anywhere on the front cover of any book.
3. On notebook paper, fully describe what you see inside the frame.

Sketch an Animal!

(Pages 65 and 66)

1. Cut off the two strips below.
2. Choose one strip and cut apart its boxes.
3. Glue the boxes to your other page in order.
4. On the lines next to each box, explain how to draw what is pictured. Start with drawing a circle.

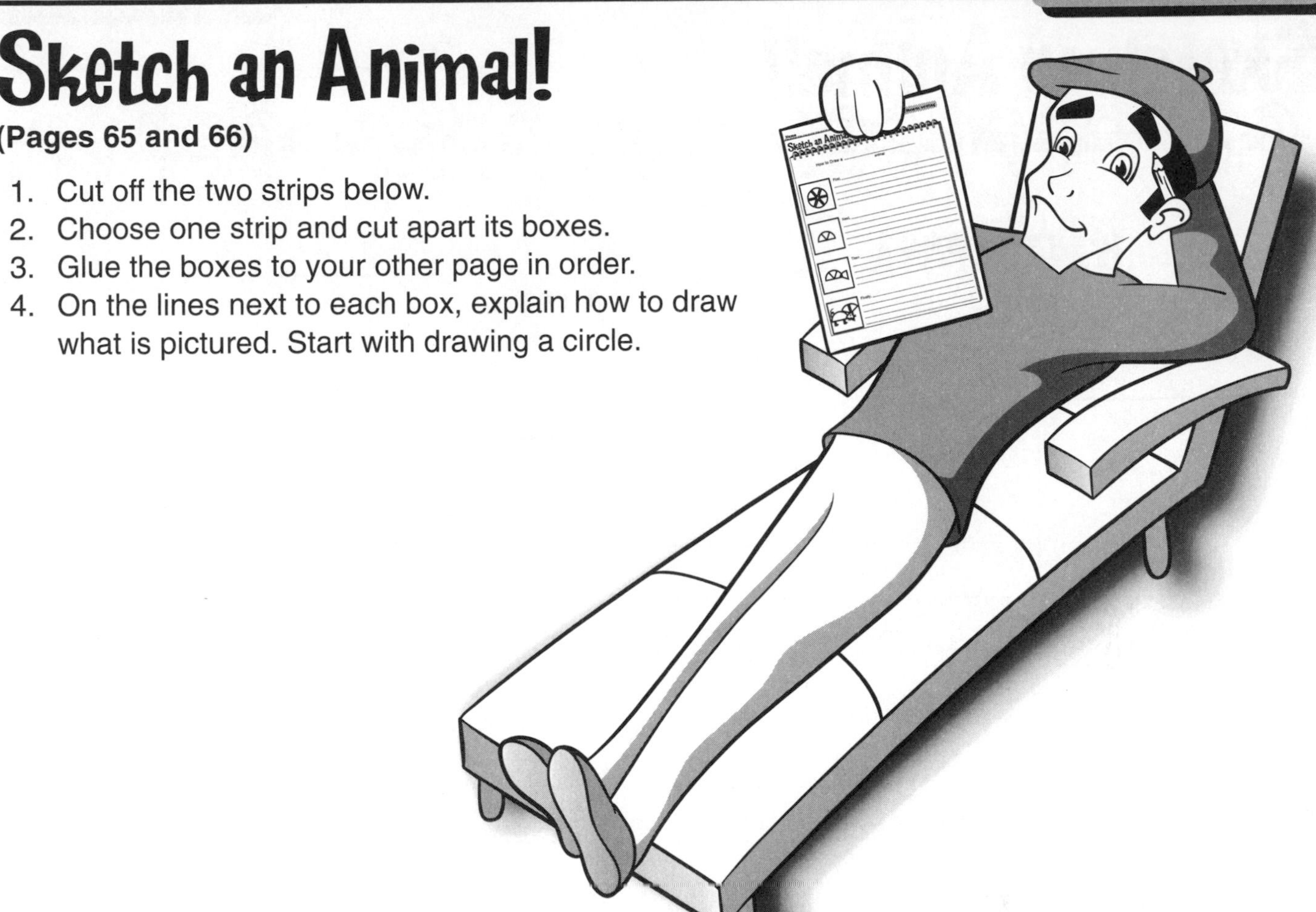

How to Draw a Fish	1	2	3	4
How to Draw a Mouse	1	2	3	4

Name

How-to writing

Sketch an Animal!

HOW TO DRAW A ______________________
animal

FIRST, ______________________

NEXT, ______________________

THEN ______________________

FINALLY, ______________________

 Note to the teacher: Use with "Sketch an Animal!" on page 65.

Name

What's the Recipe?

Choose a topic from the thought bubbles and write it on the card below.
List the needed ingredients.
Write a paragraph of directions. Use *first, next, then,* and *finally* to show the order of the steps.
Use another sheet of paper if you need more space.

Make a New Friend

Keep a Friend

Cure Hiccups

Cheer Someone Up

Be a Good Babysitter

How to ______________________________

____

Ingredients: ______________________________

____

____

Directions: ______________________________

____

____

____

____

____

____

____

Name

Launch It!

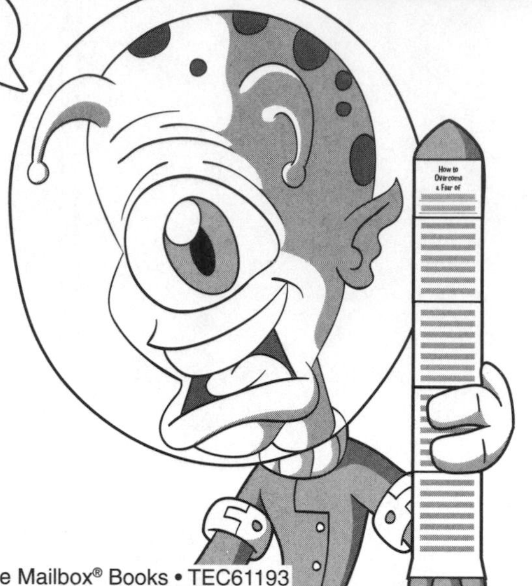
I'm scared of heights!

1. Cut out the rocket parts below.
2. Think of something that scares you. Write it on the rocket's nose.
3. On each corresponding part, explain what you could do to overcome your fear.
4. Glue the cutouts to another sheet of paper to form a rocket.
5. Use your thoughts from the rocket to write on notebook paper a paragraph that tells how you could overcome your fear.

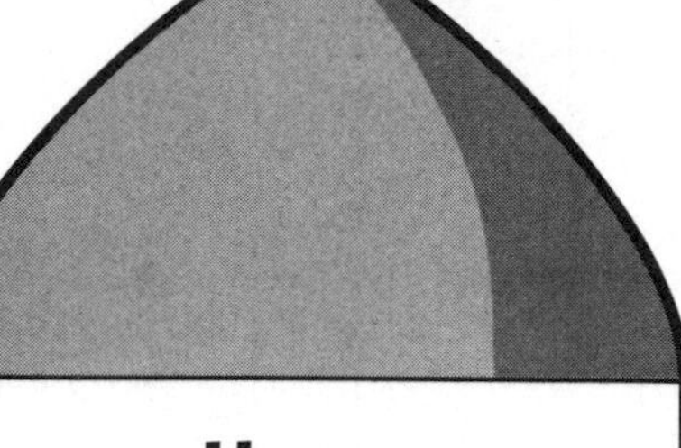

How to Overcome a Fear of

____

____

First, ____________________

____

____

____

____

____

____

Next, ____________________

____

____

____

____

____

____

Then

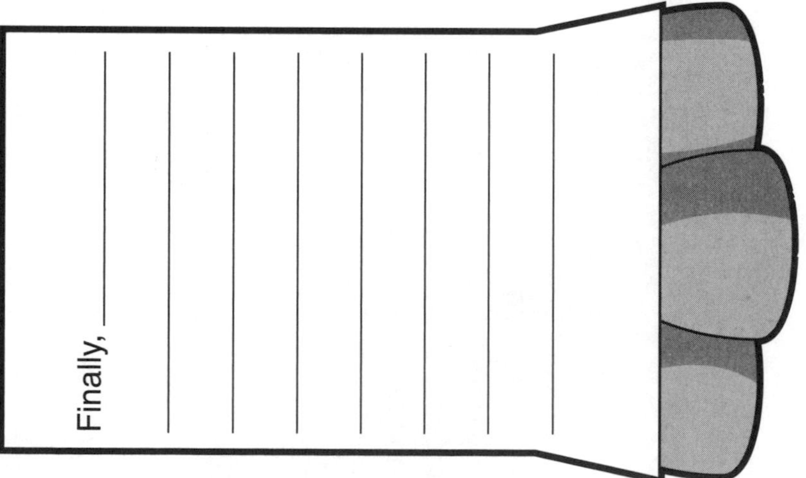
Finally,

Chat It Up

(Pages 69 and 70)

1. Cut apart the cards below.
2. Choose a topic card and glue it in the box on your other page.
3. Based on your topic, choose the cards that support your argument.
4. Glue each card on your other page and then answer the questions.
5. Use the organizer to write an essay on a sheet of notebook paper.

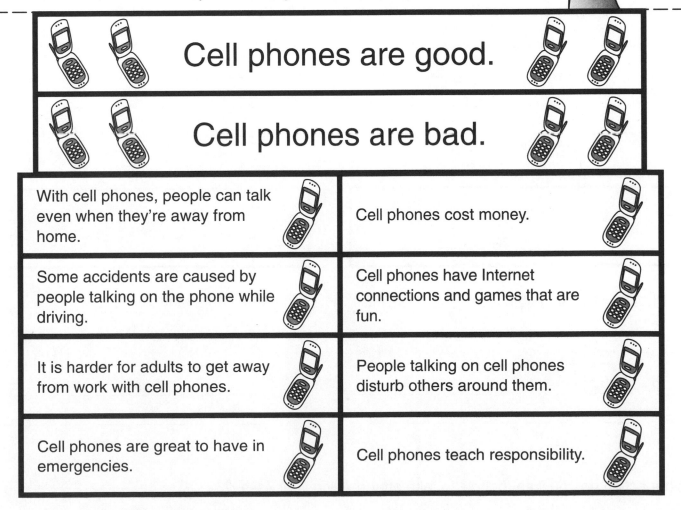

  Cell phones are good.  

  Cell phones are bad.  

With cell phones, people can talk even when they're away from home. 	Cell phones cost money. 
Some accidents are caused by people talking on the phone while driving. 	Cell phones have Internet connections and games that are fun. 
It is harder for adults to get away from work with cell phones. 	People talking on cell phones disturb others around them. 
Cell phones are great to have in emergencies. 	Cell phones teach responsibility. 

Name

Chat It Up

TOPIC:

SELECT

REASONS:

A.

What are some examples?

1. ______________________

2. ______________________

B.

What are some examples?

1. ______________________

2. ______________________

C.

What are some examples?

1. ______________________

2. ______________________

D.

What are some examples?

1. ______________________

2. ______________________

What action do you want people to take after reading your essay?

____

 Note to the teacher: Use with "Chat It Up" on page 69.

Swing Into Action!

Read the topic and complete the organizer. Then use the organizer to write an essay on another sheet of paper.

Topic:
Write a persuasive essay about something you want changed at the school cafeteria.

____

Audience: ______________________________

Opinion:
What action do you want taken?

____

____

____

____

Hot Buttons (Write your top three concerns or important issues.)	**Your Points** (Explain how your opinion helps each important issue listed.)
1. ____________________	____________________ ____________________ ____________________
2. ____________________	____________________ ____________________ ____________________
3. ____________________	____________________ ____________________ ____________________

Conclusion: (Write what you want the audience to do.)

____

____

Name

Playground Problem

1. Read the problem and its two possible solutions.
2. List the pros and cons for each solution.
3. Circle the solution you feel is best.
4. Write a persuasive essay on another sheet of paper. Use your organizer to help you.
5. Cut off the organizer. Glue it to the back of your work.

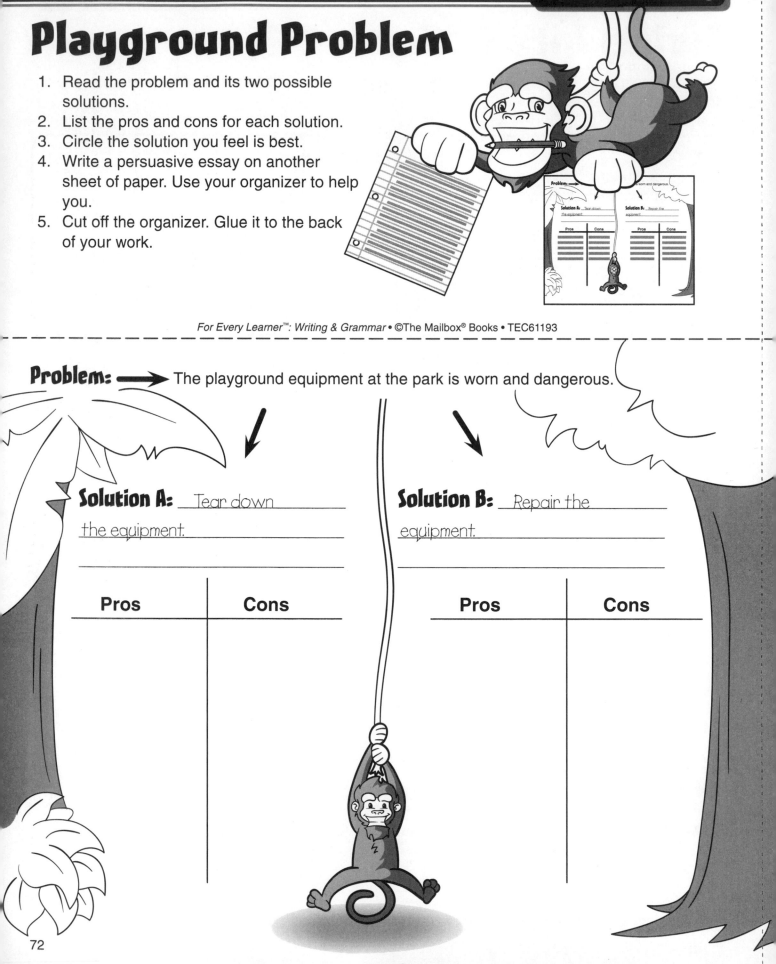

Problem: ⟶ The playground equipment at the park is worn and dangerous.

Solution A: 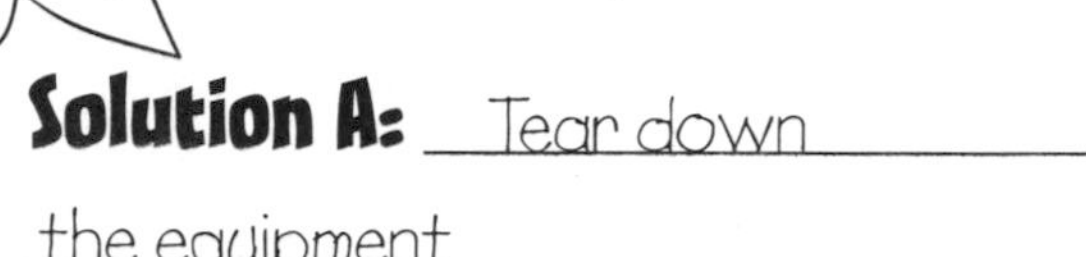
Tear down the equipment.

Solution B: 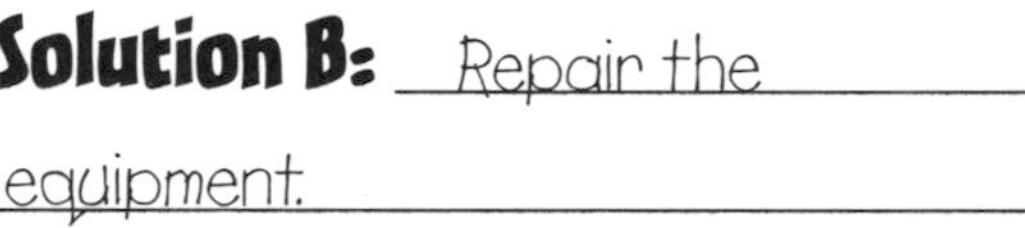
Repair the equipment.

Pros	Cons

Pros	Cons

Score a Goal!

(Pages 73 and 74)

Object of the game: to vary how sentences in a paragraph begin so they are more interesting to read

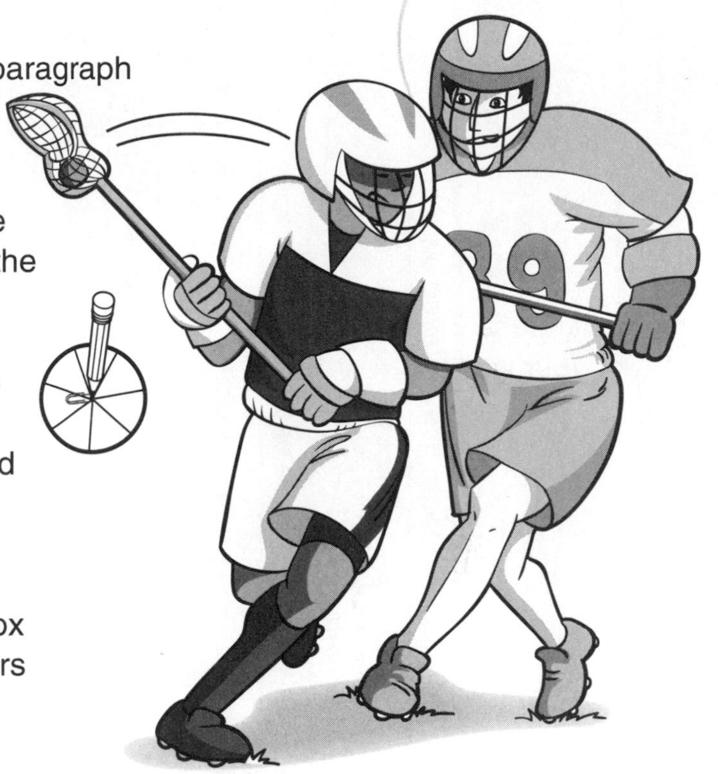

Directions for two players:

1. Cut apart the gameboards on your other page and the answer key and spinner below. Turn the key facedown.
2. In turn, use a pencil and a paper clip to spin the spinner. Read the set of sentences on the gameboard that matches the number spun. Then color the box of the sentence that should follow the boldfaced sentence above it.
3. If you spin a number you have already spun, your turn is over.
4. When you and your partner have colored a box for each pair of sentences, check your answers with the key. The player with more correct answers wins.

Answer Key for Score a Goal!

1. A
2. B
3. A
4. B
5. B
6. A
7. B

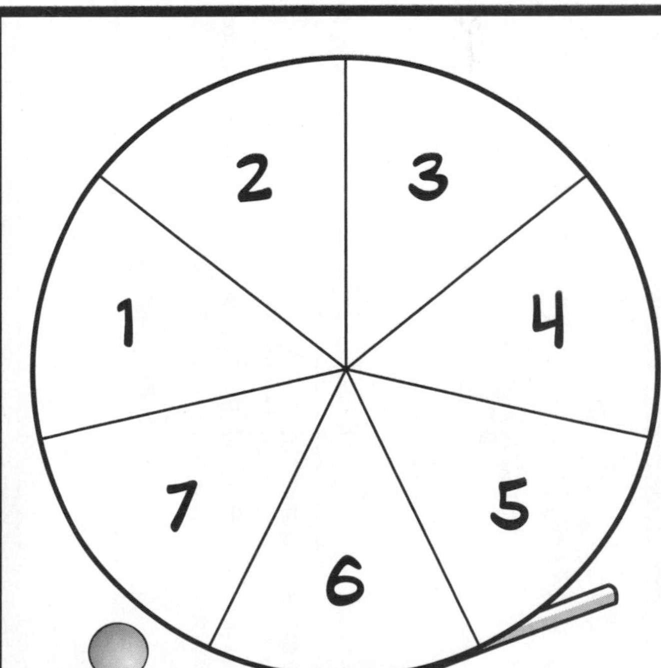

Score a Goal!

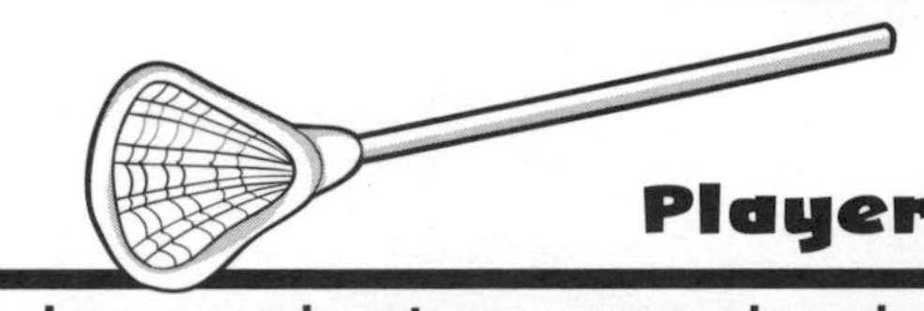

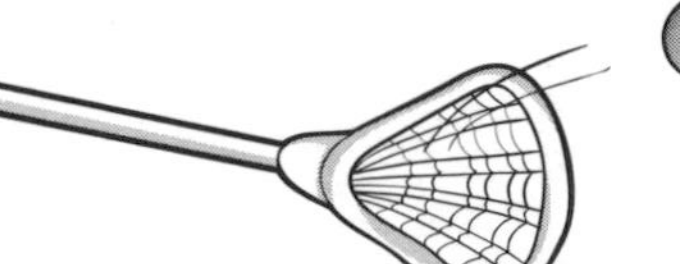

Player 1

1. Lacrosse is a team game played on a field.	
A. The object is to score points by throwing a hard rubber ball into the other team's goal.	B. Lacrosse is a game where players score points by throwing a hard rubber ball into the other team's goal.
2. Players use unique equipment.	
A. Players use special sticks, not their hands, to throw the ball.	B. To throw the ball, players use special sticks, not their hands.
3. Only one player can touch the ball with his hands.	
A. The goal keeper is the only player who can touch the ball.	B. Only the goal keeper can touch the ball.
4. A lacrosse player's stick has a unique design.	
A. A lacrosse player's stick has a net pocket on the end.	B. Each player's stick has a net pocket on the end.
5. In boys' games, players wear more equipment.	
A. In boys' games, players must wear helmets, face masks, padded gloves, and a mouthpiece.	B. Boys must wear helmets, face masks, padded gloves, and mouthpieces.
6. In girls' games, players wear less equipment.	
A. Because body contact is not allowed in girls' games, players wear only a mouthpiece.	B. In girls' games, players wear only a mouthpiece because body contact is not allowed.
7. This game is very old.	
A. This game, first played by Native Americans hundreds of years ago, is now a popular sport all over the world.	B. First played by Native Americans hundreds of years ago, lacrosse is now a popular sport all over the world.

Goal

Player 2

1. Lacrosse is a team game played on a field.	
A. The object is to score points by throwing a hard rubber ball into the other team's goal.	B. Lacrosse is a game where players score points by throwing a hard rubber ball into the other team's goal.
2. Players use unique equipment.	
A. Players use special sticks, not their hands, to throw the ball.	B. To throw the ball, players use special sticks, not their hands.
3. Only one player can touch the ball with his hands.	
A. The goal keeper is the only player who can touch the ball.	B. Only the goal keeper can touch the ball.
4. A lacrosse player's stick has a unique design.	
A. A lacrosse player's stick has a net pocket on the end.	B. Each player's stick has a net pocket on the end.
5. In boys' games, players wear more equipment.	
A. In boys' games, players must wear helmets, face masks, padded gloves, and a mouthpiece.	B. Boys must wear helmets, face masks, padded gloves, and mouthpieces.
6. In girls' games, players wear less equipment.	
A. Because body contact is not allowed in girls' games, players wear only a mouthpiece.	B. In girls' games, players wear only a mouthpiece because body contact is not allowed.
7. This game is very old.	
A. This game, first played by Native Americans hundreds of years ago, is now a popular sport all over the world.	B. First played by Native Americans hundreds of years ago, lacrosse is now a popular sport all over the world.

Note to the teacher: Use with "Score a Goal!" on page 73.

Name

Woof! Woof!

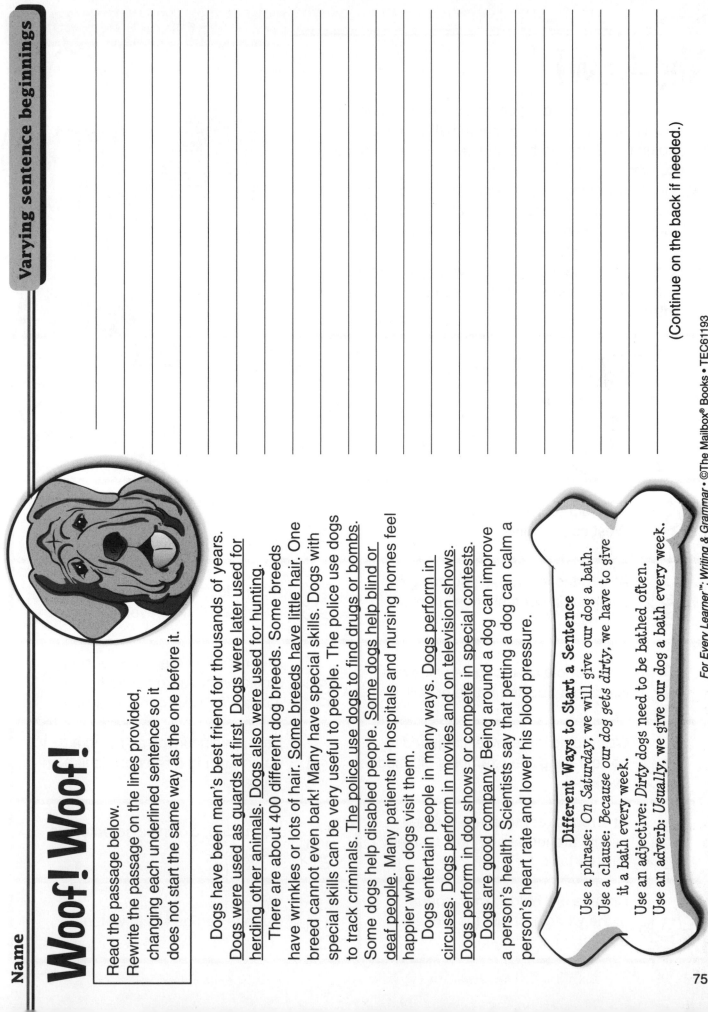

Read the passage below.
Rewrite the passage on the lines provided, changing each underlined sentence so it does not start the same way as the one before it.

Dogs have been man's best friend for thousands of years. <u>Dogs were used as guards at first</u>. <u>Dogs were later used for herding other animals</u>. <u>Dogs also were used for hunting</u>.

There are about 400 different dog breeds. Some breeds have wrinkles or lots of hair. <u>Some breeds have little hair</u>. One breed cannot even bark! Many have special skills. Dogs with special skills can be very useful to people. The police use dogs to track criminals. <u>The police use dogs to find drugs or bombs</u>. Some dogs help disabled people. <u>Some dogs help blind or deaf people</u>. Many patients in hospitals and nursing homes feel happier when dogs visit them.

Dogs entertain people in many ways. <u>Dogs perform in circuses</u>. <u>Dogs perform in movies and on television shows</u>. <u>Dogs perform in dog shows or compete in special contests</u>.

<u>Dogs are good company</u>. Being around a dog can improve a person's health. Scientists say that petting a dog can calm a person's heart rate and lower his blood pressure.

Different Ways to Start a Sentence

Use a phrase: *On Saturday,* we will give our dog a bath.
Use a clause: *Because our dog gets dirty,* we have to give it a bath every week.
Use an adjective: *Dirty* dogs need to be bathed often.
Use an adverb: *Usually,* we give our dog a bath every week.

(Continue on the back if needed.)

Name

Yee-haw!

1. Cut apart the heading cards and the sentence strips below.
2. Fold another sheet of paper in half to make two columns. Glue one heading card at the top of each column.
3. Read each sentence in order and notice how it starts. Sort the sentences under the corresponding headings.
4. Glue the sentence strips in order under the corresponding headings.
5. On another sheet of paper, rewrite the sentences that have the same beginning so each one starts in a more interesting way.

 Same Boring Beginning	 Off to a Super Start
 At a rodeo, the spirit of the Old West comes alive.	 A rodeo is a sport that gives cowboys and cowgirls a chance to show off their skills.
 At a rodeo, cowboys and cowgirls compete in contests to win prize money.	 At a rodeo, there are rough stock events and timed events.
 An example of a rough stock event is riding a bucking horse or bull.	 At a rodeo, contestants in rough stock events earn points from the judges for their form and skill.
 Calf roping, steer wrestling, and barrel racing are examples of timed events.	 Barrel racing involves riding a horse around three barrels like an obstacle course.
 At a rodeo, contestants in timed events are judged by how fast they finish a task.	 At a rodeo, clowns also entertain the crowd.
 Rodeos are held in many parts of the world, not just the United States.	 Rodeos can be fun to watch.

Answer Keys

Page 7

1. Women in the 1800s had (few) rights compared to men.
2. When (any) woman got married, the husband would then own (all) property she had.
3. (Most) colleges would not admit (any) females.
4. Women could not vote in (local), (state) or (national) elections.
5. (Some) women thought they could do nothing to change (this) way of thinking.
6. Then (several) women arranged a (special) meeting in New York to discuss the (unfair) matter.
7. Starting with (that) meeting, (popular) support for giving women (equal) rights began to build.
8. In 1920, the (19th) amendment was added to the Constitution of the United States.
9. (This) amendment gave women the (important) right to vote.

19 adjectives

Which One(s)	What Kind	How Many
𝍸	𝍸 IIII	𝍸

Page 8

What Kind	Which One(s)	How Many	Not an Adjective
amazing brisk crunchy friendly green miniature noisy steep three-sided	that these this those	50 nine several some three two	America anxiously cheerfully France hungrily

Sentences will vary.

Page 9

Singular (S) or Plural (P)	
S	1. "The Chore-o-Matic helps (me, us) do dishes quickly!" exclaimed Robbie.
S	2. This machine is awesome because (it, they) folds clothes perfectly.
S	3. "(I, We) no longer have to clean my room!" shouted Kendra.
S	4. (You, He) should tell your mom that it will vacuum the floors, Robbie.
S	5. Matt is sick, so (he, they) let the Chore-o-Matic take out the trash.
P	6. Now that (she, they) have the Chore-o-Matic, Kendra and Matt can relax.
S	7. Tell your dad that this machine will help (him, them) rake the leaves.
S	8. Kendra overslept, so (she, they) had the machine make the bed.
P	9. "The Chore-o-Matic helped (me, us) mop all the floors," said the janitors.
P	10. Now the students want the machine to help (her, them) with homework!

LET'S MAKE A CLEAN SWEEP!

Page 10

1. The basketball bounces, and the players dribble it.
2. The players on the team practice hard, and we support them.
3. Roger is the star of the team, so the coach relies on him.
4. She is the team's biggest fan.
5. Robert said, "Help me guard the other team's star player."
6. The cheerleaders bring team spirit and shout about it.
7. Britney is the head cheerleader, so she tells the others what to do.
8. "I hope we do well during the game today," said Britney.
9. "You have nothing to worry about, Britney," said Robert.
10. "We are the ones who should be nervous," replied the players.
11. Robert and the other players worked hard, and they won.
12. "You are the best!" the crowd shouted to the team.

WHAT TRAVELS AROUND THE WORLD BUT STAYS IN ONE CORNER? A POSTAGE STAMP

Pages 11 and 12

Answers for 1–6 will vary.

7. A pronoun renames an antecedent.

Page 13

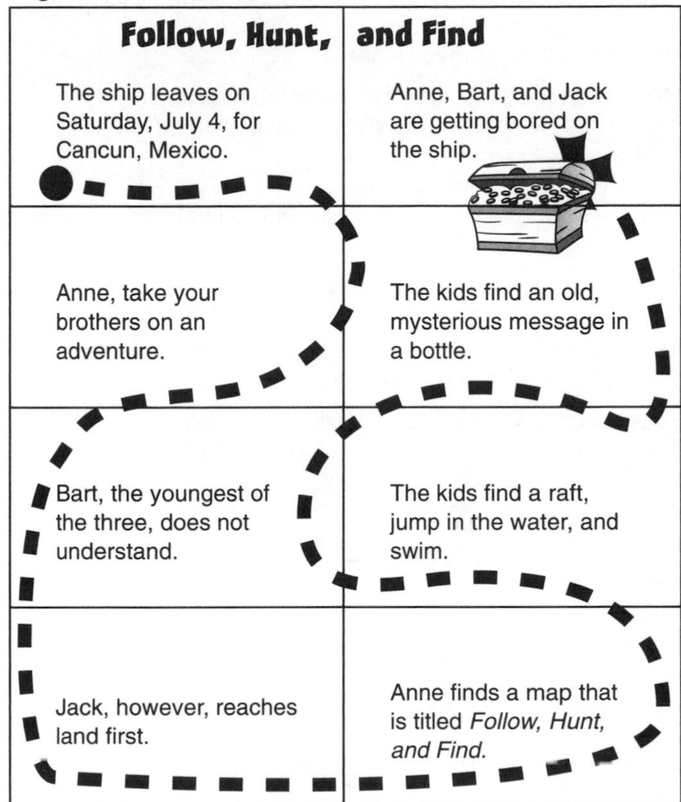

Follow, Hunt, and Find
The ship leaves on Saturday, July 4, for Cancun, Mexico.
Anne, Bart, and Jack are getting bored on the ship.
Anne, take your brothers on an adventure.
The kids find an old, mysterious message in a bottle.
Bart, the youngest of the three, does not understand.
The kids find a raft, jump in the water, and swim.
Jack, however, reaches land first.
Anne finds a map that is titled *Follow, Hunt, and Find.*

Pages 14 and 15

1. correct
2. Items in a Series; The auditions will be Monday, Tuesday, and Wednesday.
3. Appositive; My best friend, Josh, will be the director tonight.
4. Compound Sentence; Study your lines, or you might forget them.
5. Direct Address; Have you ever been to a play, Nicole?
6. correct
7. Items in a Series; She used ribbons, yarn, and cloth to make the costumes.
8. Interjection; Well, don't forget to speak clearly on stage!
9. Date or Address; The play is Friday, May 11, 2010.
10. Date or Address; The lead actor is from Atlanta, Georgia.
11. correct
12. Number; There are 1,254 people who helped with the play.
13. Interruption; I, however, like movies better.
14. Appositive; The first play, *Comma Drama,* will start soon.
15. Adjectives; The hungry, thirsty cast celebrated after the play.
16. correct

Page 17

"Do you want a horn on your saddle?" asked the rancher.
"No. There doesn't seem to be much traffic out here," replied the cowboy.

"What do you get when you cross a pig with a frog?" asked the nature guide.
"A 'ham-phibian,'" answered a young boy.

"If two rights don't make a wrong," asked Wilbur, "what do two rights make?"
"An airplane!" exclaimed Orville.

"Why are you writing so fast?" asked the teacher.
"So I can finish before my pen runs out of ink," replied the student.

A customer asked, "What is this insect in my soup?"
"I wish you wouldn't ask me," replied the waiter. "I don't know one bug from another."

"How are spiders like tops?" asked a child.
"They are always spinning!" exclaimed the child's big brother.

"What kind of ant is good at adding numbers?" asked Barry.
"An accountant," answered Larry.

Sheila asked, "Why are bakers silly?"
"Because," answered her mom, "they sell what they knead."

Pages 18 and 19

"Every strike brings me closer to the next home run," reported Babe Ruth.

"Never leave that till tomorrow which you can do today," advised Benjamin Franklin.

"I've missed more than 9,000 shots in my career. I've lost almost 300 games. Twenty-six times, I've been trusted to take the game winning shot and missed. I've failed over and over and over again in my life. And that is why I succeed," said Michael Jordan.

"I have not failed. I've just found 10,000 ways that won't work," explained Thomas Edison.

"All our dreams can come true, if we have the courage to pursue them," stated Walt Disney.

"I have a dream that my four little children will one day live in a nation where they will not be judged by the color of their skin, but by the content of their character," said Martin Luther King Jr.

"If you're going to draw a comic strip every day," commented Charles Schulz, "you're going to have to draw on every experience in your life."

"I know not what course others make take," exclaimed Patrick Henry, "but as for me: give me liberty, or give me death."

Pages 21 and 22

Bus Stop 1: "If you don't wake up, you're going to miss the bus!" Mom shouted.
Bus Stop 2: My school bus can be described as the following: loud, fun, smelly, crowded, and stuffy.
Bus Stop 3: At the bus stop, many kids talk and tell jokes.
Bus Stop 4: On average, how many students ride the school bus every day?
Bus Stop 5: "My favorite T-shirt is school bus yellow," Wally said.
Bus Stop 6: "I hope the school bus is running late today; otherwise, I might miss it," Wally stated.
Bus Stop 7: Every morning I grab my backpack, which holds my homework; grab my lunch; and run to the bus.
Bus Stop 8: Have you ever read the book 101 Ways to Pass the Time on a School Bus?

Page 23

1. "Maria's favorite candy includes the following: bubble gum, jawbreakers, and licorice," Abby explained.
2. To get to the candy store, make a U-turn at the end of Poplar Grove Road.
3. "Candy: A Sweet Guide is my favorite book!" Maria exclaimed.
4. Abby replied, "I like candy; I, however, like fruits and vegetables better."
5. What! How can you not like candy more than anything else?
6. When you eat candy, you also must brush your teeth frequently.
7. I've been eating candy since I can remember, and I don't plan to stop anytime soon.
8. "How many cavities do you have?" Abby asked.

Page 24

Some end punctuation may vary.

1. "I love to do experiments!" Professor Bill exclaimed.
2. Test tubes, beakers, microscopes, and compounds are all over his messy lab.
3. Professor Bill asked, "Where did I put my safety goggles?"
4. The assistant is absent; Professor Bill needs help.
5. Which of the following is correct: add an acid to a base, or add a base to an acid?
6. It's always a good idea to clean up after yourself; don't leave a mess.
7. Professor Bill's favorite all-purpose apron is missing.
8. "First, I need to wash my hands," Professor Bill said, "before I start the experiment."
9. "Wow, what a mess!" Professor Bill said.
10. Please buy my book titled Running a Lab Smoothly.

Answers will vary.

Pages 26 and 27

1. smells
2. call
3. buy
4. uses
5. steals
6. has
7. love
8. travel
9. chases
10. needs

Page 28

Written answers may vary.

1. plural
2. singular
3. singular
4. plural
5. plural
6. singular
7. plural
8. singular
9. plural
10. plural
11. singular
12. plural

Page 29

Present	Past	Past Participle
begin	began	begun
bite	bit	bitten
break	broke	broken
choose	chose	chosen
come	came	come
do	did	done
draw	drew	drawn
know	knew	known
see	saw	seen
swim	swam	swum

Sentences will vary.

Page 32
1. pay
2. made
3. sung
4. threw
5. swung
6. met, flew
7. dove
8. fell
9. caught, ran
10. came
11. struck
12. went, sent

Because there's a fan in every seat!

Pages 33 and 34
Order may vary.

In July, my family took a vacation, and we saw traffic signs everywhere we went.

My dad wanted to cross the tracks at a railroad crossing, but flashing lights told us that a train was coming.

Dad could have turned left at one intersection, or he could have gone straight until he came to a stop sign.

One sign we saw had eight sides, and it was red with white letters.

I wanted Dad to drive faster, but he had to obey the speed limit signs.

The sign told Dad he could make a U-turn to go back the way we came, or he could turn the van around in a parking lot.

Page 35
Answers may vary. Possible answers include the following:

A 4 Brian asked Trevor to come over and play video games, and Trevor said he would.

B 2 Brian had a new game that was hard to play, but he knew Trevor could figure it out.

C 7 Trevor loves to play video games, and he plays all of them well.

D 1 Brian prefers sports games, but Trevor likes all kinds of games.

E 3 Brian offered Trevor a snack, and Trevor said he would like something crunchy.

F 5 Brian said they could eat chips and popcorn, or they could eat cookies his mom had baked.

G 8 Brian took some cookies, but he did not take any popcorn or chips.

H 6 Brian munched on his snack while he played, but Trevor ate his snack after the game.

Page 37
1. H; Jana likes going to car races because she wants to be a NASCAR driver someday.
2. C; Drew saves most of his allowance so he can buy model racecars for his collection.
3. G; When Jana's family watches a NASCAR race on TV, they sometimes have pizza delivered to their house.
4. B; Since Jana lost her earplugs, she must buy new ones before she goes to the race on Sunday.
5. A; Although it is not supposed to rain during the race, Jana and Drew will still take their raincoats with them.
6. E; When they know they are going to a race, Jana and Drew get dressed in a hurry!
7. D; Since their dad buys their tickets in advance, they never have a long wait to enter the racetrack.
8. F; Unless the prices on food have gone up, Jana and Drew will have plenty of money for snacks at the racetrack.

Page 40
Answers may vary. Possible answers include the following:
1. When I get a checkup or need a shot, I go to Dr. Fisher's office.
2. I went to see Dr. Fisher yesterday because I started feeling ill.
3. My throat was so sore and scratchy that I could hardly swallow.
4. Whenever I see Dr. Fisher, he is always wearing a white coat and a stethoscope.
5. My little sister wants to be a doctor like Dr. Fisher because he helps people.

Pages 41 and 42
Order of details may vary.
A tornado is the most forceful of all storms.
- Powerful tornadoes can lift cows and cars off the ground.
- Winds are very destructive.
- Tornadoes can last from a few minutes to over an hour.
- Winds swirl at very high speeds.

Scientists called meteorologists study tornadoes.
- Tornadoes are studied in labs and outdoors.
- Some scientists film real tornadoes.
- Scientists hope to learn why tornadoes form.

Know what to do when a tornado strikes.
- Go to the lowest floor of a building.
- Stay away from windows.
- If you can't get inside, lie flat and cover your head.
- Park and get out of a car.
- Get out of a mobile home.

Page 43
1. red
2. blue
3. green
4. red
5. green
6. blue
7. green or red
8. blue
9. red
10. blue
11. green
12. red

Page 44
Groupings and topic sentences will vary.

A Venus flytrap is about one foot tall.
It has white flowers and odd-shaped leaves.
Each leaf has two halves that are joined.
Each leaf half has stiff hairs that work like triggers.

It takes ten days for a plant to digest a bug.
The leaf reopens when the plant is finished eating.
Each leaf can eat three meals before it dies.
Dead leaves fall off the plant and new ones grow.

A bug lands on a leaf and makes contact with trigger hairs.
The leaf snaps shut and the bug is trapped.
The bug wiggles as it tries to get away.
The leaf closes even tighter around the bug.

Page 45
like warm climates
live in South America and the southwestern United States
can live as long as 20 years
sometimes dig underground burrows for their nests
sometimes live in trees
are not usually very poisonous
cannot see very well
sometimes eat small rodents and reptiles

Paragraphs will vary.

Page 46

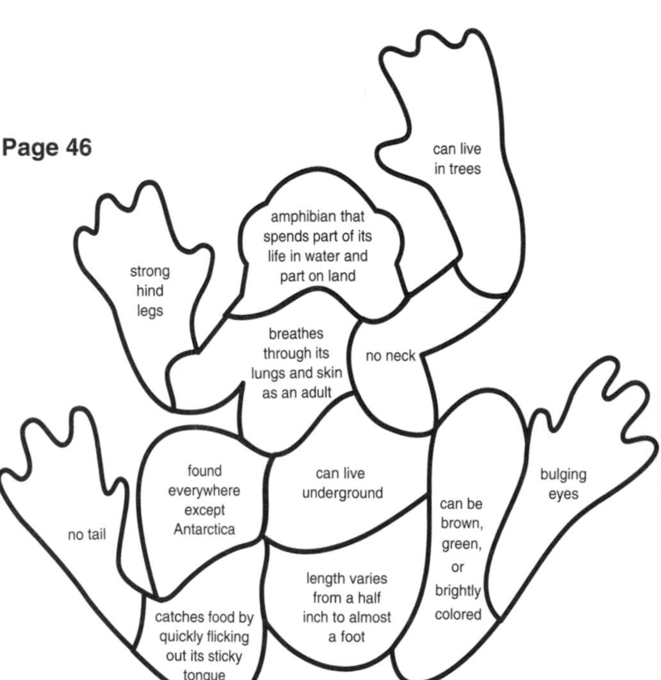

Paragraphs will vary.

Page 53
1. A
2. B
3. B
4. A

Pages 54 and 55
1. In 1767, the American colonists refused to pay the taxes put on them by Great Britain, so the British government removed all the taxes except the one on tea.
2. Tea ships came to Boston in 1773 and the colonists wanted them sent away, but the British governor refused.
3. Angry colonists dressed up like Native Americans and marched to the harbor.
4. The disguised colonists boarded the ships and dumped the tea into the harbor.
5. The Boston Tea Party was one event that led to the American Revolution.

Page 56
Underlined details and paragraphs may vary. A possible paragraph is shown.

Pirate attacks occurred often from the 1500s through the 1700s. During that time, pirates attacked ships and towns along the Mediterranean and Caribbean Seas for money and riches. Sailors became pirates to make a living or to find adventure and riches. Some pirates became famous. Pirates had a hard life filled with danger, injury, sickness, and fear of being captured and put to death.

Page 61
Answers may vary. Possible answers are shown.

See	Hear	Smell	Taste	Touch
layered	sizzling	smoky	juicy	slippery
round	searing	charcoal	salty	bumpy
seeded	popping	delicious	bacon-flavored	smooth

Name

Skills Checklist

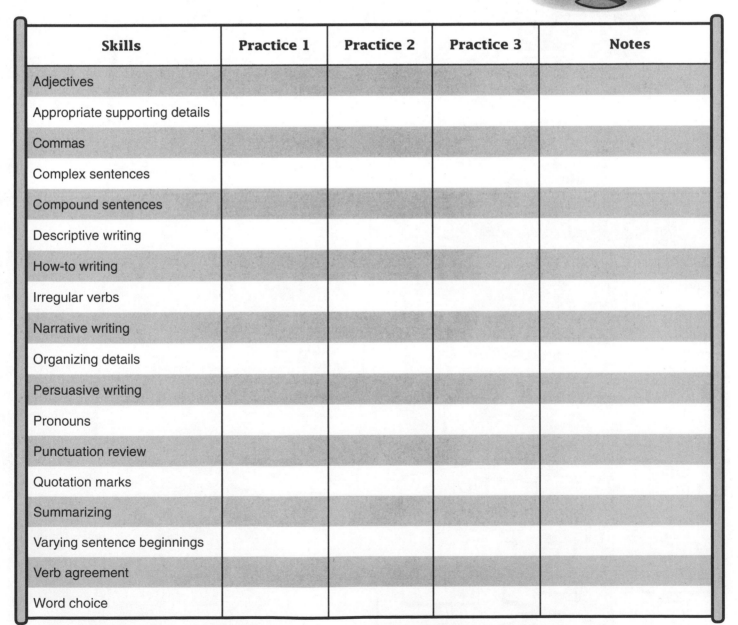

Assessment Code
M = More practice needed
S = Successful

Skills	Practice 1	Practice 2	Practice 3	Notes
Adjectives				
Appropriate supporting details				
Commas				
Complex sentences				
Compound sentences				
Descriptive writing				
How-to writing				
Irregular verbs				
Narrative writing				
Organizing details				
Persuasive writing				
Pronouns				
Punctuation review				
Quotation marks				
Summarizing				
Varying sentence beginnings				
Verb agreement				
Word choice				

Note to the teacher: To track the skill progress of individual students, personalize copies of the page. Each time a student completes a practice page, use the provided code to note an assessment of his work.

What's Inside

3 practice opportunities for every featured skill!

Formats and levels of difficulty vary!
Choose the right practice for each learner!

Table of Contents

What's Inside 3

Skills Checklist 4

Adjectives 5

Pronouns 9

Commas 13

Quotation marks 17

Punctuation review 21

Verb agreement 25

Irregular verbs 29

Compound sentences 33

Complex sentences 37

Organizing details 41

Appropriate supporting details ... 45

Word choice 49

Summarizing 53

Narrative writing 57

Descriptive writing 61

How-to writing 65

Persuasive writing 69

Varying sentence beginnings 73

Answer Keys 77

The MAILBOX®

grade 5

For Every Learner™

Writing & Grammar

3 Differentiated Activities for Every Skill

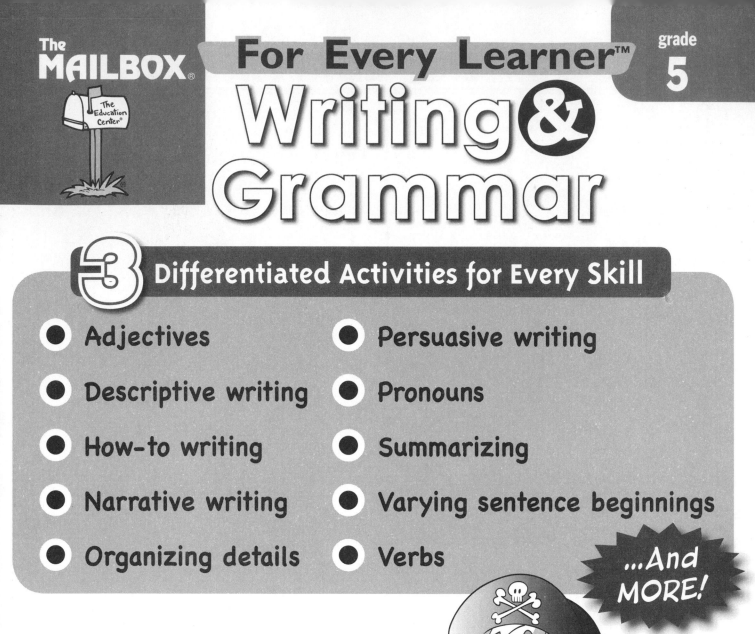

- Adjectives
- Descriptive writing
- How-to writing
- Narrative writing
- Organizing details
- Persuasive writing
- Pronouns
- Summarizing
- Varying sentence beginnings
- Verbs

...And MORE!

Managing Editor: Peggy Hambright

Editorial Team: Becky S. Andrews, Diane Badden, Kimberley Bruck, Karen A. Brudnak, Kitty Campbell, Chris Curry, Lynette Dickerson, Tazmen Hansen, Marsha Heim, Lori Z. Henry, Angela Kamstra-Jacobson, Debra Liverman, Dorothy C. McKinney, Thad H. McLaurin, Sharon Murphy, Teri Nielsen, Jennifer Nunn, Mark Rainey, Hope Rodgers, Rebecca Saunders, Renee Silliman, Barry Slate, Patricia Twohey, Zane Williard

www.themailbox.com

ISBN10 #1-56234-871-X • ISBN13 #978-1-56234-871-7

Printed in the United States
10 9 8 7 6 5 4 3 2 1